T0197187

LIVING YOUR LIFE PURPOSE
WITH THE ANGELS

SHEELAGH MARIA WRIGHT

BALBOA.
PRESS

A DIVISION OF HAY HOUSE

Copyright © 2016 Sheelagh Maria Wright.

All rights reserved. No part of this book may be used or reproduced by any means, graphic, electronic, or mechanical, including photocopying, recording, taping or by any information storage retrieval system without the written permission of the author except in the case of brief quotations embodied in critical articles and reviews.

Balboa Press books may be ordered through booksellers or by contacting:

Balboa Press
A Division of Hay House
1663 Liberty Drive
Bloomington, IN 47403
www.balboapress.com
1 (877) 407-4847

Because of the dynamic nature of the Internet, any web addresses or links contained in this book may have changed since publication and may no longer be valid. The views expressed in this work are solely those of the author and do not necessarily reflect the views of the publisher, and the publisher hereby disclaims any responsibility for them.

The author of this book does not dispense medical advice or prescribe the use of any technique as a form of treatment for physical, emotional, or medical problems without the advice of a physician, either directly or indirectly. The intent of the author is only to offer information of a general nature to help you in your quest for emotional and spiritual well-being. In the event you use any of the information in this book for yourself, which is your constitutional right, the author and the publisher assume no responsibility for your actions.

Any people depicted in stock imagery provided by Thinkstock are models, and such images are being used for illustrative purposes only. Certain stock imagery © Thinkstock.

Print information available on the last page.

ISBN: 978-1-5043-0096-4 (sc)
ISBN: 978-1-5043-0097-1 (e)

Balboa Press rev. date: 03/30/2016

INTRODUCTION

Hi beautiful soul,

When I started my journey with the angels I wasn't looking for them and truly had no idea that they even existed in the real world. It was the birth and near death of my youngest son that changed my views and my life.

My child was born and exhibited an angry red face yet no other obvious symptoms. We were home from hospital before we knew it. I however had an increasing feeling of unease that I dismissed. Over the next two days this feeling got louder and more insistent until it was a Voice – who identified when asked as 'Michael', he told me I needed to get my son to hospital – now!

The most amazing people saved my son's life only 20 minutes from death. Over the next 15 months, this experience occurred a further two times. My son's terminal heart condition brought forth operations and subsequent infection. He continued to seem fine on the outside, although the voices insisted otherwise.

So that was the start, I'm happy to tell you my son is now considered cured and is a happy healthy 10 year old bursting with life and vigour. My own life in the meantime, deteriorated and I spent the next two years trying to get myself back on my feet. I spent a spell homeless with my children, and endured much heartbreak. The voices insisted this was all part of the plan and I was learning skills and having experiences that would help me to help others in the future. At the time it was not much comfort to hear this!

I landed myself a job on a psychic line. It soon became clear I was no fortune-teller. The angels, as I now knew them, insisted on my sharing with people the 'how's' rather than the 'if's and 'when's. I realised that my path from the start was pupil and later teacher. I took great comfort in knowing that the people I read for though were gaining more than short-term assistance.

By now the angels had steered me to work with an American site where I was lucky enough to be able to work as a full time writer and channel. The writing was something I had always been drawn too. They brought me the most wonderful people to work with, tutor and develop. Yet still I was doing 'readings' rather than teaching.

My new husband, Mr Wright if you can believe that! Has supported me wholeheartedly. He told me he saw me as full of potential when at times it felt as though I had failed badly. He remains to this day my biggest supporter, lover, friend and confidante. It was my husband who encouraged me to share my story, of near tragedy, heartbreak and then a slow but magical climb upwards. He helped me to become the teacher and woman I am today.

I want to tell you that I know what it is like to not have anyone who believes in you. To not know if the relationship your in will last, or the job that your in is right for you, to sigh in desperation because your money is a constant struggle and you just wish life could be easier and yet – more purposeful at the same time.

So I wrote this book to share methods that work. Practical, real life methods that applied consistently WILL put you on your path. The degree to which you know you are on your path does rely on commitment and dedication but also magic, fun and joy.

Know that I champion your cause, all causes, wherever you are whatever you have or have not yet done. Know that we are one, all colours, all creeds, all statuses, and all backgrounds. It is time now to discover your life purpose, and I think I can say safely, the angels are all around you just waiting to assist.

With love and magic but above all motivation

Sheelagh and the angels

PART ONE

Chapter 1

WHAT IS A LIFE PURPOSE?

M any people think that a "life purpose" is a job or mission to help others, something that occurs at some time in the future. In many ways, this is true; however your life purpose is also occurring at this very moment in time—and you have already planned nearly all of what has happened so far.

Before you were born into your physical body, you were spirit—pure, euphoric spirit. You knew that coming down here would be a challenge. You knew also that, at times, you would want to give up and go home.

You planned your entire life with a few particular pit stops in mind. Even though some of this can feel highly challenging to our 3-D self, it was all planned in a bid to help you grow.

You see, in your light-body state, you are here because you want to gain experience across a broad spectrum. You know that "knowing about something" is not the same as experiencing it. In fact, you know how to change a tyre, but what's actually involved—breaking down, having to get your hands dirty and change that tyre—is a completely different experience from the intellectual knowledge of the steps. In the experience of actually changing the tyre, you really appreciate the job the tyre does for you. When you combine the energetic, the emotional, and the physical experience of it, it stays with you and assists you in other ways.

3

Believe it or not, you have had thousands of lives. Some of us have had more, and some of us have had fewer. The one thing that we all have in common is that we each chose to come down here. We chose the theme, the lessons, and even the people we were going to be born around, live with, and learn from.

You chose your parents. You were given the opportunity to choose from several couples, and you knew in advance what kind of childhood you were going to have. You understood the challenges and the difficulties (often heartbreaking for some of us) that you would face. You knew who your siblings would be. You knew how often you have been with them and other relations in other times. You valued these experiences so much that you made contracts with the souls of these people prior to birth. Some of those contracts were to learn, some were to teach, and some were to balance karma from other lives.

You also have a theme running through your incarnations. Your theme is part of your life purpose. For some people, music may be a theme; for others, light work may be a theme. Whatever your theme is, you will be learning a different aspect of it, no matter what life you are in.

In conjunction with this, you also chose two life lessons, one primary and one secondary (in case you complete the first). Usually they complement each other. The life lesson you choose has not been undertaken in just this life; often, it a carryover from other lives, so you will experience this lesson from all perspectives.

For example, a life lesson of trust may have been learnt from the perspective of a victim in the last two lives. In this life, you are learning from the perspective of a teacher; in others, you may have been a perpetrator or an observer. Regardless of the viewpoint, in any life, you are challenged to explore higher perspectives. If you are truly aware and dedicated, it is possible to work through both life lessons in one life

When a life lesson comes to a closure in one area (for example, a lesson of trust in family relationships), the emphasis moves to learning about self-trust. The lesson can often be in conjunction with your career or through witnessing other situations in which you are asked to trust your higher guidance.

When we are learning about our life lessons, we may feel that we have already learnt it adequately. Your guides know your higher self's true agenda; they and your soul council have been trusted by your higher self (part of which remains watching from heaven) to ensure you do have ample understanding of the lesson before the theme changes. Towards this end, the lesson is likely to be presented to you in different ways, through different soul mates, in different subject areas, and at different times of life. It is never that you are being tested or punished; it is that your entire being and your entire soul are designed to grow and expand. It is designed to learn different facets of life and of you, thereby allowing it all to happen. So you see, lessons and interactions are neither *bad* nor *good*. At the soul level, they are designed to help you grow stronger, expand your awareness, and build wisdom.

When we refuse to learn from these life lessons, they are presented to us again. This may seem harsh, but the reality is that this particular life lesson has to be repeated until it is learnt. You will then have a reprieve before the learning starts again.

Life lessons are often considered learnt in that area, however, when we over-identify with a lesson or an energetic example, it becomes our point of attraction. So even though, from spirit's point of view, we can move on, through our very experience, we become attached to patterns of belief. The Law of Attraction has to keep bringing us more of what we identify with; this is why the angels want you to ask them to help you.

Asking the angels to help you identify whether this is a lesson or an attracted example is important because it may mean that you need some help with this. It may be that you have established a pattern of energetic identification that has been impacted by the soul mates around you. Their experience of life and beliefs can influence your energy. Below I have included a tip from the angels to help you know the difference between what is yours and what is theirs and what is attracted and what is not.

What Is Your Life Purpose at This Moment?

At this moment, your life lesson is a culmination of what you are growing through and what you are avoiding. What you are doing? How you are doing it? What pace are you following? With what energy you are you doing this? Your life purpose is the way you view yourself and the way you view others. Your life purpose is the judgement you come to and the expectations that you hold. Your life purpose is very much not *what* you do but *how* you choose to continue to do it. This, in turn, enables either more-positive opportunities to learn, grow, and flow—or less-positive examples.

Your life purpose is the tone, something that is chosen moment by moment.

Your tone is the energetic average you are emitting vibrationally as a signal to the universe. The level of this tone is what attracts soul mates, opportunities, and new experiences; if this tone is negative, it will also attract barriers and old, negative habits—and cause them to remain longer than they should. This tone also determines whether you stay where you are or move to a more comfortable level of reality.

The thing to remember is as your tone changes, so will the tone of those around you. As you do your healing work, others will be inspired to grow with you. These relationships and interactions will either evolve or these people will vibrate away from you. You cannot control this or manifest the growth for them; it is their choice when, how, and *if* they expand.

Changing your tone is as easy or as difficult as we make it. The thoughts we have are set by the thoughts we have had. Because our feelings are energetic responses to those thoughts, we will often feel at the mercy of those for some time, even as we seek to change those thoughts.

The angels have also asked me to stress that manifestation of lighter, more loving experiences can only happen after you have consistently altered your tone (a combination of your thoughts and feelings) for a period of time. If you give up too soon (because you feel that nothing is changing), then your reality cannot improve

If you do not know how to change your tone, the angels also want you to know that help is at hand. All you need to do ask them to assist you! They will either help you themselves or guide you to someone who can.

Is It a Life Lesson or an Attraction-Based Event?

When you understand that you *can* change things, you will be able to see the results more quickly. If it is a life lesson, you can shed the heaviness and be ready to flow into your next stage easily. If it is an attraction-based event, you need to identify the beliefs and patterns that keep you tied in at this level. Only then can you flow into the next stage. Until your point of attraction has changed, you would also not be able to receive any improved outcomes. Either way, you need some help in identifying what's really going on.

The Results of Changing Your Tone

When you change the level of your thoughts and feelings, you not only feel better very quickly, you also feel better about *what is*. When you feel better and more accepting of what is, it all changes bit by bit, and soon you have left "it" behind. The answers you desperately need flow in swiftly, and you begin experiencing new outcomes that prayer, pleading, and effort could not manifest. You feel lighter, and because of this, you can move on to the next level.

Tip From The Angels : to identify whether it is a life lesson or a attraction based event get a pendulum, ask for confirmation that yes you are called Bob or Joan (whatever you name is) to establish your 'yes', then ask 'dearest angels is this experience part of a life lesson?'. If you get a 'yes' then ask 'What is the energy I need to heal?' and go through these questions 'is it a fear based energy' if you get a 'yes' then ask 'is it fear?' 'is it frustration?' 'is it resentment?' if you get 'no' you can ask 'Is this occurring because of something in me that needs to be healed?' If you get a 'yes' then sit quietly ground your energy and ask your team 'what do I need to heal?'. You'll FEEL or HEAR the answer, trust them they want you to expand!

If it is an attraction based event ask the angels 'what do I need to heal in me to change this energy?'. Sit quietly and connect with your heart and FEEL where your focus has been drawn too. If you've been noticing all the lack around you or all the shortcomings of a partner then this energy flows into your life in bigger ways. Very simply it is now time to move on to 'changing your tone'.

Tip From The Angels to Change Your Tone: it takes time to change our tone, the Law Of Attraction will not allow us to swivel from one point to another. However we can do this gradually moment to moment even though it takes practice and consistency. In the end it is SO worth it.

What ever is going on please stop, and take some deep breaths right now. Focus on what is reliable and good about this moment, what can you trust in your life, who can you trust? What can you be grateful for (even if there are 100 reasons NOT to be it's time to go into gratitude for AS MUCH as you can). The angels are asking you for the next 48 hours to say 'thank you' for as much as you can in your mind, thank you for your food, thank you for your children's health, thank you for the light and the heat, thank you for the soft rain, thank you for the daylight, thank you for this book. KEEP doing this even when something occurs from the old energy. Keep going and also take some time to do the things that make you happy that are easy, such as a long hot bath or a sleeping in later in the morning. If you keep this up for 72 hours your tone, your focus and soon your point of attraction will change. Even if you have situations around you that are challenging, even heart breaking, you will change THESE situations by changing your focus on the small stuff.

From the author: 'It doesn't always feel like you are on your highest path, sometimes it feels really challenging and things are not at all clear. You may be dealing with challenges on multiple fronts and that can feel unfair. The angels told me that when you are working through old patterns being challenged, to be more patient, more focused upon your blessings and are really digging deep emotionally – this is a sign you are clearing possibly lifetimes worth of patterns and this – IS part of your highest path. I remember when it felt like everyone was against me, even the one friend and family member I trusted 'turned', it made me realise that forgiveness was vital for me to be able to grow despite the opinions of others. As I felt better about being me, new opportunities opened and the world felt lighter again. Sometimes people around you will challenge you in what feels like the worst ways, but you are capable and able to over come old feelings of jealousy, anger, and fear and you can step into the light. And when you do, that's when the rewards appear.

Chapter 2

HOW THE ANGELS CAN HELP YOU WITH YOUR LIFE PURPOSE

The angels and archangels are your guides and always with you. Some are especially assigned to you in your team with different roles and some you can call in at any time. Others will naturally be around you already aware that at certain times you asked them to be present.

You chose your parents, your siblings, even your spouses, and children before you were born. You designed 'contracts' with these members of your soul group to help you learn, teach and ultimately expand through your time on earth. However when we come to earth, we have spiritual amnesia and it feels at first as though it's all being done' for the very first time'.

Your angels hold the blue print, given to them by your soul council of 12 who rubber-stamped it and also your higher self who lives with the angels in a higher heavenly plane. Your higher self knows you won't listen to your 'self' probably for a very long time, until you realise that guides and angels are only ever passing on what another expanded version of you wants you to know.

Your life has a variety of purposes, a variety of lessons interwoven around a central theme, and you will be tested in varying ways through your experiences, your choices, your relationships, your success', and also your failures.

When ever you are finding you are stuck or blocked it is normal to feel frustrated and to need or even demand instant help or answers, And when people tell you that 'the angels are always there and always help' and you don't see immediate improvement in your situation, it can feel as though your request has fallen on deaf ears.

Your Guardian Angels are the ones that are with you all of the time. They act as a door way for you to receive guidance from other beings such as guides, loved ones, masters, and archangels.

When you ask your 'angels and guides to help' what they will do is :

1) Point you towards resources that would highlight the subject matter you need to absorb.

2) Highlight through other people the lesson you are being asked to learn.

3) Guide you towards someone who can help you either physically emotionally or with advice.

4) Guide you in quiet moments to what you really need to heal, what is being mirrored to you.

Your angels always help but they can't do it 'for you' as a rule of thumb:

1) They can't bring you money if you haven't learnt to receive love and affection.

2) They cant bring in your twin flame if you have unlearnt lessons with soul mates.

3) They can't bring you the job or the clients if you don't or cannot ask for help.

4) They can't bring you a lottery win or money if you are not a match to it vibrationally.

5) They can't make that man love you commit to you, if you do not truly love yourself and need it from others first.

Your angels and guides WILL ALWAYS:

1) Try and highlight to you where you are blocking yourself.

2) Try and show you what the energy is asking you to do ie a time to act a time to plan a time to heal.

3) Try and shield you from 'extra' lessons that you don't require but you may due to past experiences.

4) Try and highlight to you where you are not being punished you are being pushed up to the next level.

5) Try and highlight to you that you create and attract your experiences and you can always receive 'more' but you need to be specific.

6) Ensure that you have free will to accelerate step off or slow your path down.

7) Ensure you have free will to act or not as you choose.

8) Ensure that you understand 'why' certain outcomes cannot be changed.

When I am working with clients who just want or need an experience to happen or pass, they can feel strongly that it is unfair they are going through a certain difficult experience. The angels want you to know that you can heal a lot of these situations even involving others, by being calm, quiet, and accepting where you are. Only when you are not in resistance can things change.

Chapter 3

YOUR LIFE PURPOSE AND YOUR SPIRITUAL GIFTS

We are ALL born with intuition and gifts. The level to which they are present and can be developed depends on several things.

1) Our chosen 'life theme': If we are destined or designed that we would live a family orientated life without a major focus on spiritual service then although we have spiritual abilities like Every human, it may not be 'arranged' that we are going to be a professional healer, reader or mystic.

2) Our Life lesson: If our life lesson is about survival or perseverance we may have survival themes or be born into a culture or family where spiritual service is not the most important priority. Our life lessons are always accessible to us 'through our intuition' and in fact it is the 'reason' that we have intuition – so that we fulfil our lessons and expand as designed before we 'go home'.

3) The age of our soul: Put simply on the spiritual planes there are 'schools for psychic and spiritual development' you have to be at a certain 'soul level of advancement' for your gifts to 'show themselves' in certain ways during an incarnation. This is why some people develop for years and years and do not reach the

level that others are naturally born with. This is due to the agreements you made with your soul council prior to coming to earth – you cannot force your way 'beyond your soul years'.

4) Our current vibration: At different stages in our lives we have different vibrations. This is a mixture of the environment we work in/live in, and the current soul mates we have around us, where they are on their path, and how much of their energy is affecting us. Our vibration is essentially the bridge between the spirit and the physical so if your vibration is naturally high, but it's lowered because of life circumstances, or energies, then it is difficult to skip this and develop your gifts to a higher standard.

5) Our current life flow: Like the tide we have times when things are effortless and when things are not so easy. The 'flow' is affected by many energies including worldly energy. If we are going through a retrograde, or an ascension period or many people are struggling with their growth, it can impact upon the energy that you as an individual are encountering. When it comes to manifesting outcomes or manifesting spiritual abilities, if you are in a slow flow then you cannot kick this just through force, it's time to sit back and coast for a while.

The angels want you to know that the reason clairvoyance exists higher in some people than others is that they have a mission or a job to influence the overall soul awareness and growth. It's not because they are more spiritual or more worthy. The angels tell me in heavenly terms we are all spiritually gifted because we are a soul. It's like saying someone is a 'good human' if you are a human your classed as a 'good example' because it's what you are.

Those that feel their clairvoyant or healing abilities make them better, more unique or more connected to spirit are lovingly misguided. People that work in hospices, care for animals, raise a loving family and are instrumental in their own growth are as connected to heaven and their life purpose as any clairvoyant, mystic, or healer. The truth is that the ego can play us for a fool and tell us that we are more vital than any other cog, yet without every cog the wheel could not turn.

Chapter 4

YOUR SPIRITUAL GIFTS UNCOVERED

The angels tell me there is an umbrella which covers all the intuitive abilities. Bearing in mind we all have these, we also all have them for our own life purpose. So someone with amazing clairvoyance may use it to help others but essentially has this ability so that their knowledge of their own ascension is fulfilled. Nothing is more important than ones own ascension, as without this you cannot help others.

Although we all have intuitive abilities, how they present themselves to ourselves, and then for others is unique and different. Again the angels tell me there is much one upmanship or ego where this is concerned.

We are ALL connected to the universe, God, angels and guides. This is because we all COME from the universe, God, angels and the guides. We all have a soul group to which we belong. Soul mates, soul contracts, (all coming later) life lessons, and experiences through which we will grow.

Because of this the angels tell me we all have to experience all things so that Source or God grows. So we all have a team, made up of different beings, which are designed and chosen by us prior to birth to ensure we do learn our lessons, and teach our experiences to others.

To have a team of magical and ever loving beings, which aid us in listening to our higher wiser self, (which sounds like you and feels like you and is part of God him or herself). Well it would make no logical sense whatsoever that in order for you to understand your life purpose and all that goes with that, you would have to pay someone every time you needed guidance. It would defeat the object of self-realization.

If you have a team of guides and angels (and I can assure you, that you most certainly do) you also possess the ability to hear their guidance and comforting words of wisdom when you need them. Now, the 'words' and sentences that they speak are in a universal light language, not English French, or Spanish. They do not always as some mystics say, 'speak them to us' using words.

In fact, the guidance always comes in energy form, first and it comes 'to you' through two different channels, either through the backs of your chakras, or in through your auric field.

Your chakras face 'outward' like flowers on a stem, and yet the vortex of energy does not 'start' at your back bone, rather it goes through the etheric realms and the energy of your guides angels and higher self is 'pumped through them' so it feels like it is coming 'through you' – indeed it is but it's not actually coming 'from this version' of you even though it may feel like that.

Your auric field has 22 layers. Think of yourself as an onion. Each of these layers represents another facet another dimension of you. It's a raindrop from the raincloud which is your soul, which is higher expanded and would never fit into a physical body such as yours.

Your angels and guides stand either in the 7th level of your aura, (or closer if you have invited them close) or they hover 'above your soul star' which is like the garden gate at the font of your house. When the time is right either at soul level or invited by you, they will flow as an orb and sometimes 'open out' into their light body through your crown and into your aura. Their messages come like waves of energy 'into your aura' and often clairsentients feel the energy first.

There is much talk of fortune tellers predicting your future, the truth is that there are always around 7 possible futures at play, and these can change in the literally half a second. For this reason, the angels are inviting you to create your future by understanding your gifts, and how to use them.

What Are My Gifts & How Do I Develop Them?

You came here with a unique blueprint and a 'rough' idea of what you would be learning. Your gifts are the doorway to making sure you do learn and grow as you intended too, and they are uniquely perfect for you.

The angels tell me that humans perception of 'how clairvoyance works' and 'how they think it is' for other people is essentially flawed. The idea that clairvoyants and mediums go around seeing and hearing completely externally is one that can earn them a lot of kudos for the wrong reasons, and can also prevent people (you and once upon a time myself) from thinking we are or have anything special to give.

Every person in the world has some intuitive ability, and every person in this world is encouraged to develop their ability so that their life's purpose can be fulfilled.

Your gifts are unique and cannot be compared to anyone else's gifts. For a long time I have seen people tell me 'they will only go on the stage if spirit proves to them it's real' and then these talented people never use what God intended them to use and share.

Just as eggs can be used to make a million different dishes, not everyone was meant to be a spiritualist medium or clairvoyant. There are actually many types of clairvoyance and many different types of 'reader'. I hate to tell you despite exclamations, there isn't one that is better or more talented than another.

I often see people telling me how amazing a certain medium is, and that's wonderful but there are so many variations of energy just because someone doesn't see spirits walking around everywhere does not mean they are not gifted. In fact some of the most talented healers/channellers I know don't exhibit their services for fear of not being able to 'prove' what they are getting,

Your gifts – honestly will also be affected by a variety of energies, from the energy of the place where you live, to your thoughts and feelings. Even the stage you are at, the soul level, the teacher who is teaching you, the people you are reading for, or the situation you are getting personal guidance on. It's also likely to be a mixture of all 3 'clairs, and it's very unlikely that you are purely clairvoyant, audient cognizant or sentient.

Just as developing your 'core muscles' will also tone up your buttocks and your thighs, so too will developing your ability to feel will tone up your ability to see and hear.

Am I a Clairsentient?

For the purposes of this chapter I am working with the angels rather than an institutions definition of what is and isn't energy work. The angels tell me that energy comes in through your crown or through the back of the chakras. Very often your Guardian angels will 'waft' messages in energetic form into your aura and you may 'feel' the energy come in often but the angels tell me that Clairsentients acutely 'get the messages first' where a clairvoyant takes the energy up to the third eye and processes it, or an audient takes it to the temples or the ear channels.

Your are likely clairsentient if:

You tend to use the words 'I feel … ' preceding a statement.

You feel the energy in a room and either like it or not.

You feel comfortable or not comfortable in presence of someone.

You make your decisions based on how you feel in response to something.

You have previously 'felt' that something was going to occur of a certain nature, and it did.

The angels tell me that to develop your other psychic senses it's important not to skip over your strongest. By tuning into the angels and asking them to communicate with you, rather than getting annoyed because you are not seeing or hearing what you feel you should, try tuning into your third eye and 'feeling' what you are seeing. Or tuning into your hearing and 'feeling' what you are hearing. This is how I developed my now accurate Clairaudience and voyance many years ago.

You may well 'feel' the presence of your angels and guides either as an emotion, (such as feeling highly reassured when Michael is with you) or feeling 'tickles' or 'tingles' around your body. You may feel cold, or warmth in relation to certain energies and be able to tell 'who' is with you by these sensations. It is entirely possible to develop other gifts such as mediumship or speech channelling from a sentience point of view because you are obviously acutely sensitive, It's also important if you are Clairsentient to understand empathic connections and how these can influence your energy field, you will find out more about this later in the book.

Am I Clairaudient?

Clairaudience means 'clear hearing' and it is true that some mediums and clairvoyants healers and psychics have heard or do hear externally. Generally most clairaudience occurs internally in the mind, as we sense the 'resonance' of the voice 'behind' our mind voices. The language and the tone is different to what we ourselves would use. Often when sharing an audient message the sitter will exclaim that the words or phrases are what their loved one or what they themselves were thinking.

It is rare but not unheard of for people to hear externally, generally the angels tell me that this happens if someone is in immediate and urgent need of assistance, or if they are rundown and open to communication. Sporadic and spontaneous Clairaudience as with any time of instantaneous phenomena is usually for one of three reasons:

1) You have an unprotected aura and you are open to different grades of energy. This isn't good because if you pick up on the wrong sort you may cause yourself problems.

2) You are being 'woken up' by your team and hearing them or seeing them clearly is part of the initial plan. When this happens it usually only occurs for a short amount of time as it takes them so much energy to infiltrate our heavy vibration. Many would be mediums feel 'upset' that they have 'lost their gift' when in fact it was only ever a starting point.

3) You are being visited or guided by loved ones that have passed or an energy that requires your help. Often this is because they have a particular message that they want or need you to convey in order for them to be able to move on. Many people see what I call 'haunted house' energy, which are orbs and shadows. We would not personally class this as a gift but more of an occurrence. Some people see fairy or elemental energy as orbs or hear laughter. This is lovely and your guides will often catch your attention in some way, however it is not normal for this to continue and it's not an indication of your true gift.

Putting it simply, although you do have the ability to connect with your team, it is unlikely that they will go through hoops to help you if you are not personally committed to raising your vibration and growing. It's also important to understand that it's a choice we have to heighten our gift; they can't do it for us.

Am I Clairvoyant?

There are different types of clairvoyance. We have 'sleep clairvoyance' where you see loved ones, angels and beings in your sleep. We have precognitive sleep clairvoyance which occurs in the same way. There is also 'life path clairvoyance' which is the good old-fashioned fortune telling type. It is only as accurate as the energy is stable – not very long term. There is Spiritual Clairvoyance where you are able to connect with your own guides and angels. Or for someone to pass on messages of guidance and elevated perspective. There is also energetic clairvoyance where you can see auras, orbs and other types of consciousness.

If you are a clairvoyant you may have occasions where you do see externally, flashes of light from the corner of your eye, light bursts, and shadows are all very common. Mental clairvoyance is much more common and is the most normal way for your team and loved ones to communicate.

Am I a Medium?

There are some outstanding mediums out there. Mediums basically are focused upon survival evidence. 'Psychic mediums' who read tarot cards are not 'mediums' in the strict sense of the word. Mediumship is something you are born with. Although you can develop it to some level, most true mediums are born not developed. A lot of people feel if they can't give strong survival evidence they are not a medium. The truth is you are correct to some degree, however there are also different types of mediums and painting all mystics with the same brush never works.

Survival mediums – connect with the mental body, in the auric field and their guides or the spirit directly will communicate with them in this way. They are likely to be able to give evidence which the loved ones can validate.

Mental mediums are usually clairvoyants that have some accuracy with this. They will not always be able to offer the high level of accuracy that survival mediums can, simply because they are 'not wired' that way. It doesn't mean they are not accurate or talented it's just a different auric set up. Mental mediums may have a particular affinity with human souls and yet may deliver a different type of message. For example they may give' present life' situation messages rather than 'Joe had a wife called Joyce and they lived at 89 Smith Street'. The angels tell me again to pass on the gift you have, and is the best one to develop rather than tying yourself in knots to be something you are naturally are not.

There is also open trance and physical mediumship, which is another area all together.

Am I A Healer?

Everyone can become a healer. But it doesn't mean you are destined to be one. I have lost count of the number of reiki therapists who tell me they were born to heal, and yet they have many personal issues they are not over coming and growing through. A born healer will have 'hot hands' and they are rare. They don't need a modality to help them to help them tap into this, they heal just by their presence.

Healers are as clairvoyant as anyone else. They are usually the last person to tell someone they have a mediumistic message for them. They are likely to be found at the back of the room supporting someone with a physical or emotional problem.

The angels tell me lovingly that everyone has the ability to heal so essentially we are ALL healers. It is wonderful there are so many methods which allow you to learn your own life lessons whilst sharing the gifts and energy that you've learnt. However they remind us that our priority must always be to grow and open ourselves first before attempting to help anyone else.

Am I An Angel Reader?

Oracle cards are great fun and everyone can use them. Everyone can connect with their angels and 'the angels'. Being an angel reader is different to being an angel channeller which is also different to being an angelic 'speech channel'. The angels want me to highlight that reading energy remotely for someone is easy, but how you convey that energy and their messages is the difference between whether you were 'born to do it' or are 'just doing it '.

Angel readers, channellers etc are all very aware of their role, which is simply to pass on the messages the angels bring through. We are not fore bringers of doom and we do not have any special status. We are simply servants of the light and we benefit hugely personally by doing so type of work. The angels want to point out that everyone on earth has the right and the ability to communicate with angels and guides but it is down to our own discretion how we allow ourselves to pass that information on. The difference between a light worker and someone still on their path to development, is that a light worker will take no credit and will not judge another person based on what they are given or the response that they get. It comes 'through 'them but is not 'from or about' them and so the messages do not elevate or decelerate the path of the client or the reader.

The angels would like to point out that whether you are clairvoyant, clair cognizant (knowing) sentient or empathic, you have every right to develop your ability in a way that helps you first and then others after. Whether you love to use crystals, tarot, pendulums, or let them speak through you, the only thing that matters is your intention. If it's one of love and compassion for your fellow man, then yes it's perfectly okay to get paid abundantly. Then you are a light worker and it is part of your purpose.

Am I An Angel Channeller?

The angels tell me they will channel through anyone and everyone for the sake of good for the world. If your vibration is high and clear you can channel angels. Channelling angels happens in a variety of ways. You may likely have channelled angels already by giving advice which is 'sager than you are' at certain times. The angels come through the heart centre first and you are going to feel a huge sense of empathy when you channel their advice. This is different to other forms of clairvoyance because it is higher, purer and heart based. It is not necessary to have cards to channel angels and the advice is accurate but loving – always loving.

Am I a speech channeller?

Speech channellers are people who allow light beings to talk 'through them'. Some speech channellers are conscious when this happens others seem to be 'taken away' to somewhere safe as this happens. Speech channellers are born but can also be developed if your vibration is naturally high and clear.

Signs you are channelling are:

1) The advice or words are accurate for the person hearing them but are laced with love compassion and wisdom. If you are given a message that is anything but purely loving and is at all ego centred, the person may mean well but is not channelling high guidance.

2) The Posture, face shape, or even accent and language will alter if you are channelling a higher level being. Sometimes it is very obvious and sometimes it is slight, yet it nearly always happens at some level.

3) You will feel euphoric and not be concerned about the accuracy whilst you are delivering the message. Those that are truly 'born' to channel do it because of the absolute love and happiness that flows 'through' them as they are bringing through the guidance. It is literally channelling pure heavenly energy into the space. Great for the client and wonderful for the channeller.

4) You may channel a well-known archangel, or a light being that has a unknown name or is a sound or is even 'nameless'. Sometimes you may channel a group entity. (think of Abraham channelled by the marvellous Esther Hicks) or you may channel one being (think of Seth or Orin and Da Ben)

5) When you are channelling you are in a heightened state and it is important to ground and close your crown afterwards otherwise the neighbourhood riff raff may pay you a visit.

Other Types of Reader/Intuitive:

Years ago Spiritualism was the 'norm' for intuitive and energy work and much of it was steeped in 'must have' and rules. Now there are new types of mystics being born every day and whatever is perfect for you and the people you assist, is your path, your life purpose and cannot and should not be judged or compared to that of another.

The purpose of this book says the angels are not to 'clone you' as being a medium, healer or an angel reader. You are many things in many ways. You are a fantastic light being who came to earth to help others expand through your presence. You have had many different lifetimes not all of them on planet earth.

You have many different attributes at this moment, and many that you haven't even delved into yet. In past lives you are likely to have been a mystic, a healer or many other roles. But what is vital is that you don't fall into the trap of only identifying yourself as having a life purpose if you are 'one of the above'.

Having said this, if you are highly empathic, but work a 'day job'. You are a practitioner of some kind, but are having money problems. If you are a past life reader, but can't find your soul mate. It does help to understand that wherever you are housewife or CEO is valid. It's important and vital to the ascension of those around you. Some of the most 'clairvoyant' people I have met (I'm mother to some and married to one) do not 'do a spiritual day job' on the surface.

Other types of readers may include:

Empathic animal communicators
Prosperity coaches and healers
Twin flame and soul mate readers
Medical intuitive
Emotional reconnection specialists
Karmic healers
Intuitive Auric readers
Fairy and elemental channellers
Relationship readers
And many more.

The important thing to understand is that you have a gift for a reason and to remind you once again:

1) Learn what your life theme is and live it fully

2) Learn what your life lessons are and grow through them

3) Identify soul mates and help each other expand

4) Understand where you have gone 'off path' and get back on

5) Receive guidance for yourself in all topics and family and friends

6) Be an example to those around you

7) Receive all the abundance love and fun (yes fun) that you can whilst you are on this amazing earth

8) Be an inspiration to others and also to yourself

9) Form a lasting connection with your amazing and loving team and be the most amazing version of you yet

10) Expand as a soul, and contribute to the ascension of all humanity

11) Feel magical and have a great time

Sheelagh Maria says: Right now we have so many different types of pathways for energy workers that it's amazing. Remember that what you 'think' fits you at the beginning may not be your soul's true path, but rather where you are starting. Whatever energy is easiest for you to connect with is part of your path, and whatever way of connecting (healing, cards etc) makes you happiest is also what's meant for you. When you are on your souls path, things happen effortlessly and easily and do not have to be forced. Remember you are meant to enjoy the journey.

Chapter 5

HOW THE ANGELS CAN HELP YOU

The reason I wrote this book is that there is nothing else like it out there. Not only do I want you to understand that you have a life purpose, I want you to receive clarity and help living it. In this chapter the main archangels are going to come forward one by one and explain how they want to help you.

Read down through the descriptions and the channelled messages and see 'who jumps out at you'. There will be a reason for it, I promise!

Archangel Michael – Spiritual Protection & Clairvoyance

Archangel Michael is the best (and most handsome) of the archangels. He personally saved the life of my magical son Michael. Michael is depicted as the warrior dressed in flowing robes of blue or purple brandishing a sword and looking very fetching in a suit of silver armour. Michael is the angel of strength and protection but also truth and honesty. If you are drawn to this angel it's likely that:

A) You have areas that feel unsafe to you and you want to feel strong and safe.

B) You have past lives affecting you emotionally or mentally that are blocking your purpose and gifts.

C) You are not seeing what you need to see in an area of your life so you can progress.

D) You are being affected by the energy of others, and it's preventing your life purpose.

E) You have the gift or could have the gift of clairvoyance and it's time to develop.

Michael is very strong; he's also very direct, blunt and straight to the point. Out of all the angels he does not mince his words with platitudes. If you need advice, this is a great angel to ask but he won't tell you want you want to hear. His directive is to get you doing what you came here to do. He will assist you if you ask him at every turn. He will also point out where you are not helping yourself to expand.

Michael is perfect to help you cut cord with those that are holding you back. To clear blocks to abundance and happiness and to manifest higher levels of intuitive ability and clairvoyance.

Archangel Gabriel – channelling, communication and honesty:

Archangel Gabriel is to me a beautiful, strong, and energised female angel. Most famously depicted as the angel who told the shepherds of the impending birth of Christ, 'she' is dressed in robes of white and gold and carries a trumpet to signal her communication speciality. Gabriel can help you if you are having issues communicating with loved ones or co workers, she is also excellent at helping with communicating with children or young people. If you are drawn to this angel it's likely that:

A) You are able to channel angels through writing or speech.

B) Your life purpose includes communication and truth in some way.

C) You are having issues speaking your truth.

D) There is something you are not saying through fear.

E) You have an area where honesty is important.

F) It's time for you to see things differently.

Working with Gabriel is wonderful if you are experiencing stuckness in matters of negotiation or agreement. Ask her to open the channels of communication so that all the parties know or hear what they need to hear to get things moving again. Gabriel can also help dissolve ties that are no longer working. She can also help you to heal blocks with abundance and receiving. She helps you to focus on what your highest priority is. And even helps you to identify when you are procrastinating.

Archangel Raphael – healing of all areas:

Famously the angel of healing his beautiful light energy is perfect if you are having issues in any area. Of course he can help you to heal physically. But one of his greatest strengths is helping you to identify and understand the root cause of your physical disease so that you can change what is flowing in. Raphael works closely with emotional toxicity and he will highlight to you where fear or anger is blocking healing on any area. Raphael can also help you to release past lives, which are affecting you in your current one. In subjects such as money and success Raphael's green light can melt away stagnation blocks and yes cords too. If you are drawn to Rapahel it is likely that:

A) You have a situation, which is causing blocks in your life.

B) You have energy from others affecting your path.

C) It is time for you to take responsibility for your life and your growth.

D) Your feelings and focus are keeping you stuck.

E) There is something you are missing in your evaluation that will help you to heal.

F) Your blocks to money or love have an energetic root cause.

I love to work with Raphael to help identify what's really at play. When I work with someone who cannot manifest for example a loving relationship or a successful career, it is often an issue of trust or hurt that is lingering in the aura and is preventing fresh energy from flowing in. I recommend understanding that his tone of communication is through 'feeling' rather than words. His energy is light. Don't feel that it has to be heavy and serious to be effective. Heaven itself is full of light and love, so angelic communication in this way is normal too!

Archangel Metatron – Miracles and changes of direction divine timing:

If you are drawn to archangel Metatron it's time for change. Metatron is a beautiful angel who is known as the 'voice of the almighty'. His energy is very solemn and wise but loving and true. He speaks like Michael directly but has the energy of a wise sage teacher who has waited till he is asked for his advice and guidance. Metatron helps us in times of transition and he helps those who are truly ready to step into their purpose and ready to take on their role as creator. If you are drawn to Metatron it's likely that:

A) Your path has a change coming and it may feel scary at first.

B) Your path involves others and it's time for you to allow them to carry their own load.

C) Timing is at play and you are feeling impatient.

D) Timing is at play and you can't avoid this any longer.

E) You need a miracle and that my friend is you!

F) It's time to understand you too are part of god, and you are a powerful creator.

The 'tone' of working with Metatron is always 'meant to be'. He shows up when things are at a tipping point and he has absolute confidence in your ability to do what you agreed too. Put simply he helps you to step into your power and remove the blinkers from your eyes. He works with people that are catalysts. Those who are ready to do more than just talk about change but want wholeheartedly to BE the change. I love this angel and he wants you to know if you area reading this, it is safe to expand and yes he means YOU!

Archangel Zadkiel – Transformation And Fun:

If you are drawn to this gorgeous white haired angel then you are ready for some positive change, but in a light and loving way. When I connect with this angel he makes me smile widely because he brings a sense of joviality to the proceedings. He knows that you are challenged and he knows that you aren't sure what is the next step. He wants you to relax and trust in your own guidance which says 'feel the fear, let it go and go for it anyway'. This angel shows up when you are surfing 'into' your life purpose It may involve re-education, movement and decision-making. He comes not to hold your hand but to cheer you on from the sidelines and remind you that yes you did sign up for something bigger. Zadkiel wants to free you from the limits of your human perceptions. He knows full well how scary and worrying some of life can be, however he doesn't want you to use that as an excuse for not doing what you came here to do. And honestly you already knew that didn't you? Zadkiel is perfect to call upon if:

A) You are experiencing changes in your relationships and you are frightened or frustrated.

B) You want to see progress and yet you don't know what step comes next.

C) You know in your heart that something is coming but you don't know 'what' or 'who' that is.

D) You are ready SO ready to step away from old beliefs and transform into the light being you truly are.

E) You can see beyond the old stories that you or those around you are holding onto – they just don't feel the same to you any more.

As we come to a close on this 'Billy idol' lookalike angel he reminds you that you have the power to attract and improve anything he just wants you to know this for yourself.

There are 1000's of Archangels but I would now like to introduce you to some of the best to work with to help you practically on your path.

Archangel Jasmine – Family And Relationships:

She looks like a Persian princess with gorgeous pink and gold robes and has a fizzy loving energy. Jasmine is the archangel of communities', families and co-operation. She wants nothing more than to see harmony, evolution and people working things out together. She is the perfect angel to work with if you and your children. (Often step children now days) Or you and your in-laws cannot get along. She is perfect for working out the bits you can't agree on with loved ones. She will help them to see things even for a few moments from another point of view. Archangel Jasmine works best if you call on her before a conversation or communication that could have far reaching results.

Work with her by: Lighting a pink or yellow candle and having a jar of beautiful flowers. Call her in and ask her to help everyone concerned agree on the salient points. Ask her to establish harmony in the home and reinstate ease and flow in relationships.

Archangel Haniel – Manifestation And Empathy:

Archangel Haniel understands that you have a desire to manifest new opportunities but she asks you to be patient and above all happy with where you are. When we feel blocked or prevented from moving forward our aura becomes full of static which makes it difficult for our angels to assist us. Working with Haniel is a magical experience and she will help you to tune in and understand when it is the right time. Haniel also helps you to have empathy with people that perhaps are not sharing your perspective.

To work with Haniel:

Invoke the angel of the moon at a full moon or new moon and write out the areas that you would like help with. Then holding a clear quartz ask Haniel to neutralize any beliefs or patterns that are preventing you from manifesting the next step. 'See' the moons lunar energy entering the quartz crystal and now place the crystal over your third eye. 'See' this golden energy entering into your third eye and melting away any perspectives that prevent you from taking action in the right and timely manner.

You can also ask Haniel to remove any blocks or defence mechanisms between you and those that you are trying to work with or alongside She will gently erase any expectations they have that are preventing heart to heart communication and co operation from taking place

Sheelagh Maria suggests: when working with angels they will often know who is best and right for your energy. Even on a day-to-day basis this can change. Often you may work with one angel in the morning and another in the afternoon. Sit and simply ask 'who is with me now' and you will 'see' a archangels name or get a colour which you associate with that angel. Let them guide you, they know you well.

PART TWO

Chapter 6

INTRODUCTION TO THE ANGELS

A ngels come in all shapes in and colours, and although they are considered human they actually are nothing but consciousness. They are neither male nor female but some of the angels are more male in their energy and likewise some are more female.

There are a dozen books out there, which introduce you to the archangels, but I am focused upon the angels that are working with YOU directly in this book. Put simply you will have the following surrounding you.

Your Guardian Angels:

When our soul was individualized we broke off into groups. When we did this, we were accompanied by larger higher vibrating piece of source, our guardian angels. They are with you every life time you have ever had, or ever will have, and they carry you into your body, and stay with you for every second of every minute you are in your physical realm.

Your Guardians angels are numbered between 2 to 7 and they are very like you in your energy. Some of your Guardian angels have been with you since the beginning. For some people that are destined to grow and expand an awful lot, sometimes their angels will change as their vibration gets higher and closer to the light. Unlike your guides, your Guardian angels don't have their own learning to do; they are focused entirely on you. In fact their very existence is down to you. That's how unique and special you are to them. Your Guardian angels will recruit other help for you as and when you need it. Some are of the angelic variety and some are not. To ensure you have a wide variety of help any time you need it.

When you pass back to spirit, your Guardian angels will start lifting you out of your body in the days before, so that the passing is less traumatic. This is often when people have a sense of 'getting their affairs in order' before they go back home to their loved ones.

Your Archangel

When you became a individual soul, you went to a Soul College type of training. This realm of training equipped you for your lifetimes in a variety of ways. The archangel whose college you went to, is overseeing your path as we speak right now. The Archangel whose realm you were in is a lot like a loving headmaster who has a working knowledge of the progress of all the pupils in their care. They are aware you may work with many other teachers, yet ultimately they take responsibility for your progress.

Along with your Guardian angels, you will also have certain archangels that come into your life without prior arrangement. This is because ultimately we are all one and the whole of heaven benefits when you step into your purpose. For this reason, do not be surprised if another archangel comes in with a message during readings for you. Or you find yourself particularly drawn to an archangel for a period of time. Very often your own archangel has arranged for this to happen, knowing that you need specialist help, not in their area of expertise.

There are currently more archangels in existence now than there ever has been. A lot of them have not been interacting with humanity before. Because humanity is on the precipice of great change. We have caught the attention of beings that worked with other races, and now we are lucky enough to be on their radar.

When working with the archangels it is important to clarify that it Is an archangel of light that you are working with. As where light exists also does darkness, so simply asking for the 'best most loving and highest archangel to work with me at this time' is the best advice. Or to ask directly, 'are you from the purest light of source'? If for any reason you feel worried, concerned or judged then simply ground yourself, call in archangel Michael to remove the presence back to source and all then is well.

Speciality Angels:

Along with our other angels, we will also have groups and bands of speciality angels who are with us for many different reasons. For example if you are having some issues within your home and family, you will attract a band of family and domestic angels. Who for a time will live along side you in your home to help smooth things over. You will have certain bands of angels with you already but here are some of the speciality angels you can ask for and you will learn how they can help you.

Psychic Development Angels: you can ask for your own group of psychic development angels, they will come in and guide you to the people and material that can help you develop to the next level. They will help you know when to take great care of yourself, and make life style changes that will elevate and speed up your purpose.

Abundance Angels: These angels are wonderful! They will guide you to the materials and information to help you understand better the nature of abundance. Many people say they need abundance, but the abundance angels want you to understand you receive abundance by FEELING abundant in many areas already. It's possible they will help you appreciate the abundance of love that you have in your life. The abundance of free time you have so that when you feel appreciation of what you already have you can attract many more kinds as well.

Health And Well Being Angels: These angels are wonderful if you are feeling off key or drained. They will guide you to make healthy choices. Although remember they can't force you to eat better or exercise more, but they will put options in front of you to help encourage you to live your best life. The well being angels will also hint to you that certain people may not be best for your long term emotional or mental wellbeing. They will also bring you materials to educate you on the importance of loving and compassionate thoughts towards yourself. They are a great bunch of angels to request when you are feeling low, ill or poorly. They will guide you to the right health professionals and can also work with speeding up the diagnosis process. They can also work with the angels of those around you to support you better as you heal.

Life Purpose Angels: Well we had to mention this one didn't we? The life purpose angels aren't concerned with 'forever' or your 'job title in one year' they are concerned about your path NOW. They will be focused upon steering you onto your highest path so that you fulfil your souls purpose. The life purpose angels are great to call on if you are at a cross roads in career or business and you don't know which way to go. They will help to show you your options, if more education or skill gathering is needed for your next step. They may bring you a professional to help you, or guide you to the healing that is needed for your next step to be revealed. They can also help you to understand what is NOT in your highest path, and often they will highlight a relationship or a habit that you need to let go of so that your highest path can reveal itself.

Business Angels: I love these guys, they will work with you like a management team to ensure you receive the right clients and the right opportunities for your business. What I love about the business angels (and I work with them closely) is that you can ask for the different components. For example you can ask for a web marketing specialist (yes really their dial up speed is fast) you can ask for a Marketing Angel, a Soul Client Angel, a 'get me more foot fall' angel. All of these beings will either guide you to people in 'the real world' that are within your budget, and on your wavelength to help you, or they will guide you to the resources so that you can help yourself. So when you get 'an urge' to take a class, register for some marketing help, or re write your website, it's your business angels hard at work, bless them.

Relationship And Romance Angels

The relationship angels help interactions of all kind, especially between the all too common mixed family situations. They will work with ex's and new partners, for the highest interests of the children, they will help transmute feelings of fear and insecurity, and they will advocate emotional growth on behalf of everyone to ensure the family set up is a blessing for everyone. The relationship angels will also convey to you when truly, a soul contract has come to an end. They will also convey to you when having an affair is not a great idea as it will only hurt you and everyone else involved more. Relationship angels do not take sides. They are there for everyone. They see the goodness in the hearts of all concerned, no matter what is playing out. Relationship angels can guide people to try healings, clearings and work on themselves. As when a relationship isn't growing as desired it's the individuals growth that needs to occur first.

The romance angels are wonderful when you want to meet your next Soul mate. We say 'next soul mate' because there is not just one for everyone. (This is covered later on) The soul mate you attract has everything to do with where you were emotionally and mentally when you attracted them. Sometimes one grows at a different rate to another. So sometimes a new soul mate is brought forward. Sometimes this soul mate is to help you see that you are unhappy, but isn't the ultimate answer. The answer is always to work on loving yourself and being responsible for your own happiness, and only then will a new long term soul mate be brought in.

I had personally been learning lessons through relationships for 2o years. When my romance angels brought my wonderful husband into my life, although we both had learning to do Mr Wright did literally come in and steal my heart. Romance angels can help you manifest the person that's right for you now, especially when you are prepared to do your own growing in order to receive them.

The Money Angels: The money angels are not the same as the abundance angels. The money angels help you in regards to how you view and feel about money as an energy. When you interact with money in a fearful lack based way, money becomes needy or unavailable. The money angels will guide you towards the clearings, resources and awareness that is needed to change often century old patterns in relation to money. They make receiving money a pleasure and keeping it feel secure and safe. They often do this by bringing examples of what your deep-seated beliefs are by highlighting the beliefs of those around you. Asking them to come join you to up level your money experience is a great idea for everyone.

The Moon Angels: Yes even the moon has her own set of angels. They are starting to interact with humanity for the first time in recent years. They are here to help us learn about emotions, sensitivity and the 'hidden realms' which exist. The lunar angels are all about the different layers of our self, and they can be called in when we are feeling anxious, frightened and need to accept our shadow side. The lunar angels understand we want to be loved and happy, yet sometimes we need to dig deeper to let go of patterns that draw events we don't want to wards us. The Lunar angels are wonderful at helping you to understand and heal these parts of yourself. They are also the angels of dreams and help you to take the next step.

The Sun Angels: The sun angels are all about warmth joy and play. They want us to love the life we have and want us to appreciate everything we have right now in order to receive more. The sun angels can be with us even when the sun isn't shining. They can bring lightness and new energy into our lives. Calling on the sun angels to increase your levels of peace and satisfaction is a great idea.

The Nature Angels And Animal Angels: These are simply put, the elemental kingdom. Fairies are spirits that don't always have names or individual status at first. Yet as they care for the flowers, the trees and animals they are upgraded and evolve to working with humans Many fairies do become guides for their human charges and they teach us many magical things. I personally have many fairies in my team along with imps, gnomes and even crystal kings. The fairies maintain the light energy of the world and they can help you manifest money, magic, spiritual abilities and love. The nature angels are always available for you to call upon and simply will come into your aura as sharp flecks of bright light that you may even see outside the corner of your eye.

So these are just a few of the speciality angels that you can call on, but never fear if you need help they are always available and your angels want you to know they are more than willing to help on every topic.

Your Angels say: We are many, in fact we are legion, a legion of love and light at your disposal in every moment and second. When you ask we answer. When you are drawn to the energy of flowers, or the moon or the sun, when you are drawn to be in nature, or to connect with crystals you are being called by the beings that belong with them. Do not worry or be concerned about the 'right energy' or 'right angels' we are all one in the same, here to support you, help you step and embrace your path and make it as magical as possible.

Chapter 7

CONNECTING TO THE ANGELIC REALM

There is a difference in angels being with you and you knowing you are connected, they tell me. They exist at the 7th through to the 12th plane of heaven and as such their vibration or their 'shake rate' is far higher and far purer than ours in our heavy dense atmosphere.

We always have our guardian angels with us in our aura. Who acts as the loving middle men between us and 'them'. They give us daily guidance in the form of emotional and intuitive nudges, feelings and thoughts.

However, being able to channel angels, or see other angels such as the archangels, clairvoyantly happens when we raise our vibration prior to attempting to connect.

It is spiritual law that when we ask an archangel to be with us they are immediately. But your own 'daily vibration' can be choc full of other peoples stuff and so it lowers the ability to know and hear and see what you are being given.

A practice to knowingly connect with the angels always begins with grounding. Grounding is essential so that you can be both high, and pure in your vibration (the tone you are sending out to the universe daily can be lower than it needs to be to connect to the angels, however it is also important that you are grounded, other wise it is like calling round a friend to help you and being up in the loft when she calls.)

Grounding

We have 22 energy bodies, which make up our auric field. Every one of these bodies is part of our soul. Our unique energy signature and our past and future lives. Think of an onion, every single layer counts towards the whole.

When we sleep at night we go 'up' the tube that connects us to heaven. Like a silver cord it extends through the ether and will not be severed until we 'die' and go home. This cord, takes us to our guides, loved ones and the higher realms where we take classes, visit, heal and play whilst our emotional and mental energy bodies process our 'daily real life'.

When our 'Spiritual' body becomes overwhelmed, angry, grieving or otherwise jammed up with human energy it leaves the safe confines of our aura and floats 'at the top' and 'underneath' the spiritual escape trap. We become ungrounded and unconnected to our physical realm.

It is possible to become ungrounded very quickly or to have been ungrounded for some time. Symptoms of being ungrounded are:

- Too many options and none of them feel right? This happens when our vibration isn't strong or stable enough for us to hear our inner guidance.

- Feeling spacey floaty and unfocused? This happens when our energy system becomes clogged with old and outdated stuff and it means we are not taking actions in accordance with our need to expand and heal.

- Feeling irritable, overwhelmed, tearful? This happens because there is no room for calm peaceful awareness, put simply it's a desire to flee.

- Feeling mentally or emotionally overwrought unable to switch off? This happens when we are receiving 'broadcasts' from those around us and we process them as if they were ours.

Being ungrounded doesn't just prevent us from connecting with our angels; it can allow other energies to come in. Attachments of different kinds cords being the most happen occur when the 'lights are on and nobodies home' only later do we realise something is amiss.

You do not need to have time to meditate to ground and here follows the methods I use to create good grounding connection easily.

To Ground Spiritually:

Put simply grounding spiritually means you actively invite you spirit to 'come bank in please' this will immediately make you calmer clearer and more connected.

1) Close your eyes and ask 'dearest spirit please come fully back into my body – thank you'.

2) Now breathe 'down' for three long slow deep breaths.

3) For added grounding thus making it easier to go ahead and connect to the angels, please 'see' a red cord coming from your root chakra and take it all the down to the centre of the earth, 'breathe away' any fear, stress, frustration or stuckness on a daily basis.

To Physically Ground:

This is for busy people who realise they are scattered and feeling out of sorts. I use this between every client and at the end of every day.

1) Take a stone that has been in the earth or take off your shoes.

2) Breathe down 'into the stone' or into the earth.

3) Open your eyes slowly and ask 'please Gaia ground me.'

4) You will feel calmer, more 'there' alert and even more clairvoyant if you should now choose to connect.

Protection

The method of protection you use is personal to you. Simply put you are protecting yourself for yourself! So that you do not pick up empathic energy, cords or neighbourhood ruffians in energy form. You are not protecting your self 'against' anything dark or scary. You are simply keeping your energy 'yours' and not handing it out willy nilly.

When we protect ourselves we 'seal in' our intuition and development 'so far' and we 'retain' all of the healing that our team has been giving us. All of the knowledge we are processing both at a higher level and 'here and now'. Do not think that you are 'in danger' if you forget. Having said that, the angels want you to be responsible with your energy in a day-to-day way. As it is normally the living, not the non physical who attach cords, send broadcasts of lower energy and interfere with our pace and flow.

I protect in 2 ways, I protect before I am 'in another persons energy' (this can be as a psychic or when you are going to be with anyone and reading or healing their energy this can also be when you are spending time with people that you know are processing things at the moment) or this can be just generally before you go onto social media or out into the world.

The second way is when you are about to open up your crown and open 'to' the universe. Even though the universe is 'good' and loving, the opposite is also true, so depending on where you are spiritually on your path it is best to assume the direct loving channel rather than any other.

When you are going to connect to any of your team (loved ones or yours or anyone else's). You also need to protect to ensure you only connect with the party intended and not energies who pretend to be something higher than they are.

To Protect When In The Company Of Others:

1) 'See' a white light coming down from the room you are in completely covering you.

2) 'Breathe golden light into the white tube' and with every exhale it goes down further and is brighter till you are encased in a golden tube of creator light.

3) Ask 'please may I be protected by Michael's angels from negative and neutral energy.

To Protect & Connect With The Angels:

1) 'See' a white light coming down from the room you are in.

2) Go to your feet and breath white light, up up up, until you reach your crown.

3) Ask Michael to protect you and connect you to the angelic realm.

4) See yourself going up up up the white tube. You will see yourself going through darkness and greyness in your minds eye, yet you will also be aware of your physical body.

5) When you see yourself in pure white light call forward the angels of your choice.

6) Come back to your physical body to converse with them.

7) Close your crown by seeing a gold crown on your head and ask for it to be shut.

8) See tree roots coming out of your feet and breathe down for two breaths.

Your angels say: When connecting with us, first, 'sit in bliss'. This means don't try too hard to force communication. Open your heart and breathe soft pink energy in through the front. Smile and really feel peaceful. The more peaceful you are when you are connected, the higher your vibration is, and the higher it will be in your daily life. The more that you strengthen your connection with the light, the stronger and clearer your awareness of us, and your other team members will become. We are excited to connect with you and be with you in this way.

Chapter 8

SOUL MATES & TWIN FLAMES

So when your soul finishes it's 'training' under your archangel, you progress to your first physical lifetime. Rarely though is this on earth. Once you have 'croaked' from that lifetime you will progress to your Soul Group. Where you will mix with souls from other planets and other archangelic realms so you have plenty of diversity to learn from.

Your soul is 'housed' within a soul group of 144 souls. Of this you have a 'soul family' of 25 souls. This soul family 'follows your progress' closely during your incarnation and will 'beam at you' what you need to learn. Often on behalf of the whole soul group and also on an individual basis.

Your soul family has a small contagion of 5-11 souls, and these are your 'soul family mates'. Your soul mates are the group you are incarnating with at this time. Every 500 years we tie up our karma with all members personally and 'swap' into another soul mate group. Think of them like a pod.

Your soul mates will be the people that you have contracts with. These contracts are not just romantic. Soul mates can actually be:

- People you have an instant and strong bond – either positive or negative.

- People that are lovers for a short time or a long time.

- People that are your enemies those that ultimately encourage you to grow.

- People that inspire you to do more be more.

- People that bring out traits in you to be over come and healed.

It is not true that a 'soul mate is forever. Think of them like a favourite pair of shoes that you bought for a special occasion or period, you love them but they don't suit you or fit you forever. However with a soul mate you always have that familiar bond, that time and circumstances cannot erode.

I work with many people who are convinced that a soul mate is their twin flame. A soul mate can be any kind of relationship including but not always romantic. You will have been other roles to each other in other lives. For example a brother in one life may be your spouse in this life.

You can tell someone is a soul mate because:

1) You instantly recognise their energy.

2) You cannot 'hate' them no matter what they say or do.

3) You act a certain way with them that you do not with other people.

4) You have vivid dreams about them when you are not in contact.

5) You instinctively know when something has happened with or to them.

6) You understand their point of view even if you don't like it.

7) You feel you can't live with them, but can't live without them either.

Soulmate Versus Twin Flame Myths:

Here are a few of the golden myths I hear from people who feel they have or are with their soul mate.

1) I can't stop thinking of him! We are meant to be! Just because you cannot get over that man does not mean he is your twin flame. Very rarely are twin flame relationships easy, it is true. However many people 'hang on' to a soul mate for far longer than their contract stated. It is inevitable if one party is not growing and expanding that your soul, who entered into this contract to expand and grow through challenges, wants to get on with the job at hand. Often this is a soul mate that has 'gone past their sell by date' with you.

2) I'm dreaming of her. And seeing her name everywhere. People extend cords when they are scared, feel angry or simply don't want you to move on. When a soul mate is going through a hard time, it is not unusual for them to extend cords to someone they had a bond with previously. Sometimes this is an ex who you haven't seen for years. But you will start dreaming of them, often vividly or seeing their name. This simply means they are going through some processing and are trying to find a firm footing. Extending a cord can transfer their energy to you and you can start to be convinced it's mean to be.

3) I know how he feels, I can heal him. It is true with a soul mate and a twin flame you will pick up strong empathic projections. Sometimes those projections are to do with the soul contract between you both. What each of you wants the other person to feel. Consider or choose on their behalf. Sometimes you feel

an 'over empathy' as if you are the only one with the power to heal them and you are secretly scared of losing them, in this case you will empathically 'take ownership' of their problems to 'keep them with you' rather than as with a true twin flame, letting them learn ascends you both and the contract evolves.

4) There are so many coincidences. He is my twin flame! True he may be your twin flame. But coincidences are simply electric magnetic energy showing up in physical ways. I have seen so many soul mate relationships that are toxic and sad. Bringing in many 'signs' for the person I'm reading for. It Is simply a determination to keep things the way they are. If you are strongly thinking of anyone for whatever reason, they will sense this and either get in touch with you, or avoid you. Like, attracts like, it doesn't always mean they are your twin.

Signs You Have Met Your Twin Flame:

Firstly I want to clarify what your twin flame is and what the purpose of this is in your life. Your twin flame was the last soul you were 'co joined with' when you 'left source.' Simply they remained in the spiritual womb with you for the longest.

The purpose of a twin flame union is ascension and for this reason if you meet your twin too soon it may not work out. Many people do not incarnate with their twin flame because the union Is so strong it eclipses the work you were sent here to do. It is a romantic notion but often not practical. It's heartbreaking and takes a lot of focus away from your real job, which is to expand so your soul group can ascend.

Your twin flame's energy may or may not be a romantic relationship. People are often far happier with a long-term soul mate than a twin flame, who mirrors and challenges you at crucial points.

I personally am married to my twin flame. Although we never went through the runner and chaser stage, they do mirror your fears and your lessons. It can be a challenge. Often you will meet your twin if you are on one of your last lifetimes. However they may not be and may be 'behind you' in terms of their souls path. For this reason many twin flame relationships can be really fiery and also complicated as one twin struggles to accept where the other is still growing.

The differences between a soul mate relationship and a twin flame relationship can be seen as:

- A twin flame can feel like your best friend and your worst enemy by turn. This is because they mirror your good points and your bad points. What comes across as fear in you may be seen as rejection in her.

- A twin flame will make you feel complete, or abandoned. This is because the energy between you both is so strong. You can be absolutely smitten with each other until you reach an ascension point. Then the gap between where you are and where they are can show itself broadly. You will feel bereft and completely 'at sea'.

- A soul mate relationship can end. And after a few weeks you feel stronger. If a twin flame relationship ends it can follow all other paths that you go down. However the point of a twin flame relationship ending is not 'that's it'. It's to help you love yourself more and embrace other types of love.

- A soul mate relationship can be damaging when it's gone beyond the contract's end, whereas ultimately a twin flame relationship is not toxic. It may be rocky and dramatic, but not toxic. So if you are in an 'on again off again' relationship it is doubtful it's your twin flame. You literally cannot be without each other even if being together momentarily drives you mad.

- A twin flame relationship can occur between strangers. Yet you may have a happy soul mate relationship in place. Some people can meet someone that they have had past lives with and convince themselves it's their twin flame. Yet usually it's a soul mate from another soul pod. They simply transfer their affection to them because being independent for a while is scary, it doesn't' mean it's your twin

- If you meet your twin flame and you are with someone else, you will find it hard to turn away. Yet there will be part of you both that is aware you are not supposed to turn everyone's lives upside down. One twin usually leaves this is because they sense that the lessons of their beloved cannot be learnt in their presence. Ultimately they love you so much that an affair just wouldn't work. You rarely have affairs with your twin you are either with them or not.

Staying with a soul mate, delays the arrival of your twin. If you stay within a toxic relationship waiting for 'the one' they cannot come. There seems to be a spiritual rule that they will only show up when you hit a certain point.

The best advice I can give you is if you are wanting to manifest your twin, be honest with yourself about what is working and what is not. Learn from it and expand. Then and only then will your twin show themselves to you.

Sheelagh Maria says: When you meet your twin it's a spiritual sexual and emotional experience. It's not uncommon to mirror their life lessons, physical discomforts and read their minds. Your twin's family may feel an aversion to you because they sense that you are here to help your beloved to grow, and if there are karmic family issues, they may sense or see change as a bad thing. Don't take this personally you all signed up for this together.

Healing twin flame relationships and soul mate relationships is something you or a specialist can do but remember it's all about growth and expansion not hanging on in there for dear life. Although you do get more than one life, this one counts and being happy is what you came here for.

Chapter 9

GETTING UNBLOCKED

So you love the idea of working with angels to fulfil your life's purpose, but hey, this is real life. You HAVE real world problems. Maybe money issues, career, romance and you need those SORTED BEFORE you can get to what god needs you to do.

The thing is, the whole point of you being here is to learn how to do it yourself. So many times people have said 'I NEED the angels to bring me money ... ' remember that as a soul you chose to incarnate to experience the spectrum of emotions and situations. You knew you wouldn't always find it easy or desirable. But you also knew you would grow through this process.

The fact you are reading this book means your life purpose probably does involve energy in some way. You are probably so empathic that you have gotten filled up with other people's stuff without realising, so this is where we will start.

If you are empathic you probably have other peoples energy in your chakras, your energy bodies and even in your physical body, so learning how to clear your chakras and your aura is absolutely vital – but first let's start with the signs that you may be blocked.

Empathic Energy

Empathic energy is 'other peoples stuff'. You can pick this up from people you love, adore, and they don't MEAN to 'infect you', it happens to the best of us. Empathic energy is picked up just from working with, physically sitting close too, engaging with by phone or Facebook, emailing or even reading a letter.

Empathic energy starts at the outer edges of the aura. Normally, however, if you are a mental empath the energy comes first into your mental body. How many times have you realised you copy the words and language of those around you? How many times have you unwittingly started believing what they believe in terms of the economy, romance and the 'state of the world'?

If you a mental empath you need to be very conscious of the power other peoples thoughts have on you.

Namely if you are not careful their thoughts can begin to affect the choices you make and the point of attraction you hold.

Exercise for clearing and protecting the mental body

The mental body is the closest to our physical body, so if left unchecked the energy can then exhibit in your physical body. And cause physical symptoms.

1) 'Create' a white room in the centre of your mind. Now ask the question 'whose mental energy is affecting me in my life?' You will 'see' or 'feel' certain people. The one thing to be aware of is that people often project thoughts 'at you' hoping you will choose or agree with them without them asking you outright. So clearing out your mental body regularly is important even vital to your life purpose gift and general over all health.

2) Once you have noted who is there, 'see' a door opening and ask them 'to take their energy with love and leave'.

3) Now see golden light streaming into your crown and 'around' your entire body (your mental body spans your entire physical body) and 'breathe' it all the way through.

Emotional empathy happens not just when we are in physical proximity. If you take part in an online conversation, or are texting someone who is upset or angry their energy also simply comes into you. The emotional body is right' after' the mental body and what often happens is that you will later on feel anger or frustration and 'decide' why it is you feel like this, if you find yourself searching for reasons why you feel a certain way it almost certainly isn't yours.

To heal the emotional body

1) Ask Archangel Raphael to be with you now, and imagine his beautiful green light shining down.

2) Ask Raphael to heal and remove anything that is not loving and positive in your emotional body (this also includes your reactions to what you have picked up or what you have produced in response).

3) 'See' green energy coming into your heart space as well, and really see it all being lifted UP and away.

4) Ask Raphael to please LIFT OUT any energy cords that were established at the time – people attach energy cords if they are needing support or are fearful, and this can mean that you continue to pick up their energy long after leaving their company even remotely.

5) Ask that a shield of love is placed around your emotional body so that this doesn't happen again.

It is important to remember that you are not 'doing anything wrong' by picking up energy from other people. It is normal and part of living a soul centred life and interacting with others and deciding who and what are 'on your wavelength' and adapting your energy accordingly.

We now move onto the part of the mind and psychic senses that other types of energy 'pick ups' can affect.

Negative Energy Cords

Imagine as a child you felt concerned or worried, and your mother seemed oblivious to your feelings. For whatever reason she seemed distracted, emotionally unavailable and it made you feel ignored, or insecure. One of the things you may well have done (because we all do it and have done it) is to attach an 'energy cord' to your mothers aura in an attempt to hail her attention.

As we live in an energy matrix, everything, and everyone is connected to everything and everyone else. Some people, that have 'seen; the matrix describe it as a 'web of light' it is also true that we are connected to everyone we love or are ever involved in.

Sometimes these webs of light become contaminated with the energy of our thoughts and our emotions. Sometimes those emotions and thoughts are not positive and even if we are not consciously broadcasting them directly to the people involved. When you think of another person, an energy cord is already in place and it can attach itself due to the emotions that you are sending' toward that person.

Energy cords that are made from or transmitting loving feelings and thoughts are always left in place and are a benefit to all concerned, however 'extra cords' are created through our thoughts and focus and are 'attached' through focus not through intention and will 'lodge within' one of the auric layers the 7 major chakras and also the physical body itself.

The Effects of Energy Cords

Negative energy cords transmute negative energy. Just like having raw sewerage pumped into your clean water supply, they cannot assist or bring a relationship closer together. Negative energy cords left unchecked can cause problems for both parties.

Negative energy cords going into the aura can transmit 'thought forms' and these will work their way into our mental and emotional bodies and be processed by us. So cords that are sending energy into these areas, will 'feed us other peoples energy levels', yet we will process the energy and 'attribute it to' circumstances in our own lives and of our own creation.

Negative energy cords that are attached in a more pointed way, usually go into the chakras and are often being attached because of an unspoken or a feeling of non validation on the part of another and can cause disharmony and also physical manifestations into your system.

Common energy cords can be established between: Parents and their children, therapists or coaches and their clients, bosses and their employees, spouses, ex spouses and even loved ones in heaven.

The thing to remember if someone is cording you is that at some level you are allowing it to happen. There is something unresolved for you to be corded to that person, some question, some situation or some feeling. A cord that is not wanted or not 'invited' by some 'lessening' of ones own defences and will just drop into the outer layers of the aura and be of no trouble.

You can tell you are corded if:

1) You start having vivid dreams of a loved one, an ex (often from some time ago) or anyone and feel 'pulled'.

2) You 'feel angry or drained' when you think of someone, and find letting go of their problems difficult.

3) Sometimes it feels easier just to 'give into' them so that they will give you some space.

4) When you see an email or text from them you feel pulled but dragged 'down'.

5) You feel an 'I ought to' or 'I should have' when you think of that person, yet you also feel a desire to keep your distance.

6) When you think of them you can only see them in terms of their fear, their need or their lack.

7) You start to use their terminology their language and not in positive ways.

8) Loved ones in heaven can cord you if they have not fully crossed over. You may start having vivid dreams where you are not able to let them go. This is unusual, but can happen if that person feels they had something they wanted to say to you before they left.

9) In laws can cord you if they feel that you have influence over their child's choices and feel unheard.

10) Friends can cord you if they are starting to call on you more and more and you begin to feel as if it's you and them against the world, but you can't go it alone.

If you are corded there is no need to worry because it's easy and uplifting to be able to sort this out and know that now, your way forward is clear.

Cords can also be attached to marriages, business', houses and homes, animals, even cars have been corded. Any 'block of consciousness" that feels 'owned' by someone can be corded if it is perceived as having a valid effect on the status of another.

How To de-cord With Archangel Michael & Raphael

There are 2 ways of de-cording. The first is to ask for it to be done, then to 'see it'. Another is to actively do it yourself, but the important thing is to ensure you are healed AFTER the cording. As when you remove a cord a hole is left in the aura, or chakra and can allow unwanted visitors or energy to enter.

1) Ensure you are grounded, comfortable and ask Michael to protect you.

2) 'See' Michael as you would picture him (we say Brad Pitt works wonders) in however way you visualise he would appear, 'Dearest Archangel Michael please remove all and any negative and neutral energy cords from my body aura and 22 energy fields and also all of my chakras'.

3) 'See' Michael pulling the cords out and see them disappearing into white light.

4) Now invite Archangel Raphael to come in and heal you, 'Dearest Archangel Raphael please heal all auric layers, chakras and energy fields from any holes, tears or other healing that's needed, please seal my energy in with pure love and white light thank you'.

5) Take three deep breaths as if you were 'breathing away the day' and on the last breath intend that you are filled with white light.

Interesting facts about energy cords

1) Energy cords can actively be used to prevent people from expanding in their own lives. If we buy into why or who we are 'responsible for' it can be perceived as a reason why we cannot expand. Just imagine if you had no blocks. Nothing preventing you from stepping into your purpose. Just what would you be ready for next?

2) Energy cords that are put onto one person can be used by either. In other words, even you are the one who is 'corded'. You can also dispose of your lower energy by transmitting it to the other person, although in this way nobody grows.

3) When you are free from energy cords people will often sense that you have stepped back. Often they will create a drama or you may have vivid dreams about them. You may even find that they get in touch through the grapevine or you hear about them unexpectedly. This is all normal because you have been 'feeding them 'energy and without it suddenly they may, for a short time feel adrift.

4) No relationship/partnership ever gets stronger because of cords being present. The ties of love, compassion, trust and intimacy are separate to anything established out of greed or need. So when you cut cords, ultimately you are always giving someone the opportunity to step into their life purpose and learn to create and attract from a place of joy.

Sheelagh Maria Says: 'I remember meeting my husband and suddenly becoming very upset half way through the day. There was no logical reason for it and later on I discovered something had transpired at work exactly the same time I had felt a surge of emotion. The angels shared with me that people can attach cords and we can pick up empathic energy through time and space. I have even picked up a medical condition for a short time, through someone I read for on Facebook. It's a natural part of being in a body. At some level everyone is connected to others, even those they don't know. Although cutting cords is effective, what is more important is keeping your focus on positive thoughts, counting your blessings and being in allowance of where others are. Also remember that people that attach cords are only doing what is natural, we all get scared, the angels are sharing with me right now that if you protect yourself and ask that no negative cords be allowed to attach they cannot be. No positive loving cords will ever be cut and your guardian angel would make sure of this.

Chapter 10

EMPATHY AND HOW IT PREVENTS YOU FROM DEVELOPING

B eing an empath is something that is very normal and natural. Everyone is an empath at some level. Empathy can allow us to understand what's going on for someone else. It can help us to really understand and even grow through understanding another persons 'story'.

However what can happen is that when you are picking up on not just feelings, but thoughts, beliefs and patterns of those around you, your own life can be aversely affected. For example you may be experiencing a life lesson of 'trust' and be nearly 'through it' in one area, however by listening and over empathising with a friend who has also had 'trust issues' your lesson continues and you start to attract evidence which perpetuates the problem.

Over empathising with someone does not help you or them. It means that you 'come down to' their point of attraction, and can actively go backwards on your path. It's important to understand that life lessons are meant to be learnt, and over come so that you can also have abundance, happiness and purpose. If you are so busy processing other peoples areas of growth you don't get to do so much fun stuff for yourself. They also get stuck at their current level and nobody benefits.

How to tell if you are Overly Empathising with someone

1) You become aware that their situation feels like yours because when you are not with them.

2) You feel hopeless, despondent and flat after being with them, and it can take days to get back to your normal self.

3) You begin to dread seeing them or hearing their latest instalment.

4) You realise that they feel lighter and more motivated after being with you and you by turn feel heavier and defeated.

5) Your path was going well, but now evidence is mirroring there's.

6) They start to talk about 'we' and 'us' when referring to their problems in your company.

What can you do about this?

1) Check that they haven't corded you. This is normal and easy to find out. Sit quietly and ask Archangel Michael to open your third eye. Ask Michael to 'show you' who or where you are corded. You may feel your attention is being drawn to your stomach, your heart or your mind. Without judgement of that person or of your own part, simply go through the simple de-cording process.

2) Establish better protection before you are with them or respond to them via social media, text or in person.

3) Listen with compassion for a short amount of time. It's then perfectly okay to ask the angels to ask them 'so what's your next step?' Affirm that you see them in a position of being capable. And you do not attach over much importance to their current

stance. It's a stop off point but is also ultimately their creation and their choice.

4)   Understand what kind of empath you are. This means you have more information so that you know ahead of time what kind of energy can 'find it's way in' and hopefully you can catch it before any energetic chaos is wreaked.

What happens when empathic energy is affecting your thoughts

Empathic energy can also be sent to you direct in 'mind waves' or 'psychic thought forms'. These are literally conversations that someone is having 'with you' without your consciously having it with them. The effect can be that you find yourself agreeing to, or feeling as if you 'should' take on the thoughts, perspectives and viewpoints of those around you even though you really know it doesn't benefit you or them.

These 'invisible conversations' happen when someone is trying to impress upon you their belief that they are right and that you should choose, agree with or think what they do. We again have all done this, and if you find yourself 'having inner conversations' with someone and yet avoiding having the 'real thing' it's a sign that you are being affected adversely by psychic thought forms.

The effect of 'thought forms' are that you can feel 'compelled' to adopt a viewpoint that doesn't serve you or ultimately them. Removing these can allow both parties to begin to grow and be accountable for their selves; this in turn can herald relationships and communication improving.

To remove empathic and psychic thought forms

You are going to work with Archangel Michael for this too, as he is able to see what is yours and what is theirs and is happy for you to call upon him to untangle any webs.

1) 'Dearest archangel Michael please show me whose 'thought forms' are affecting me at this time'.

2) Note any family members, friends, co-workers even animals who pop into your mind. They may be 'shown to you' if you are a highly visual person or you may feel who is affecting you.

3) 'Dear archangel Michael please remove the thought forms and empathic energy that is affecting my thoughts and perspectives and please infuse my mind with love and protection.

4) Now 'see' golden energy coming in through your crown and see this energy brightening as it melts away anything which is not truly yours.

5) Note over the next few days if there are any unspoken questions, or attempt to convince you to adopt another way of thinking.

<u>What kind of empath are you</u>

Study the following categories to find out what kind of empathic 'gifts' you have and how these can be used to further your understanding of your life purpose and your spiritual gifts.

Emotional empathy: The most common and certainly at some stage affects everyone. As an emotional empath you will feel strongly 'in tune' with certain people and you may also feel very 'sympathetic' towards their life circumstances. If you have perspective over what is yours and what is theirs this is brilliant as it can help relationships become closer and can also form common loving bonds.

However, if you are feeling overly responsible, put upon or even feeling angry or stressed and 'its not yours' it's time to see that its likely causing other issues unseen for you as well. For example emotional pick-ups drag down your whole point of attraction and can affect your relationships, your finances even your physical health.

To use emotional empathy to your benefit, be aware of who makes you feel uplifted, who makes you feel drained and simply spend time with them accordingly. Also make they are aware that you are their friend, loved etc, but also use your 'inner warning system' to know when they are putting energy your way instead of taking on their own growth. Use this as an opportunity to send 'angels to them to help them' and even talk to them about their own purpose clearing and heightening their vibration. You are of far more use to them with an elevated perspective rather than being a trouble-shooter who isn't able to truly serve.

Mental empathy: Have you ever realised that you are thinking along 'new lines'? Have you realised your memory has got sharper or decreased? Have you realised that your point of view has changed entirely, and you didn't notice it? Have you also started to 'see things' the way that those around you see things and it's markedly different from how you used to feel? Mental empathy can be a great tool if you are around motivated, highly sensitive people, on the other hand if you are spending time with people that are stressed, overwhelmed and low, it can actively create chaos in your own life.

The angels suggest as a barometer, when you are with people to note the words that they use. Do they use open high vibrational words when discussing their life and their path? Or do they talk in closed terms about dead ends, limits and lack of movement? The words that people use in their conversations often denote where they're thoughts are currently 'at' if you note that they are not open to new pathways and opportunities and you know you are a mental empathy. Intend to step back with your own conclusions and take your time before agreeing or seeing things 'their way

Plant and nature empathy

This is not as common. Some people naturally feel connected to plants, nature and animals because they are not 'contaminated' by mass consciousness. However some people go even further and literally 'feel' things from the earth's point of view. Have you ever felt outrage, deep sadness or mistrust when you see 'the way' people treat our beautiful planet? Have you ever felt a deep sense of sadness when you look at the forests, the oceans or the wildlife in them? What you are picking up on is Gaia's sadness. As the way that humanity does not love its natural birthright abundance. If you are a nature empath you will often feel the need to send healing to a particular place, and you will also 'feel' when some kind of purging or upheaval is going to happen.

A wonderful way to use your gifts is to learn animal or devic (elemental) communication, and also to receive healing from trees you can even give healing from nature, from the Oceanic animals, and life forms, the flowers and goddess energy. If you are a natural nature empath you will also find meditating in nature or spending time in nature does wonders for manifesting a stronger connection with your gift and also accelerates your life purpose.

Place Empathy

Likely you are picking up on energetic imprints left by other tenants and other times. Even if your house Is brand new the energy of the land it's built on may contain trace energies from other times. No non-physical energy can truly 'harm' you, it just doesn't always feel good if you have this incredible gift.

Using place empathy is perfect when you want to improve the energy of where you are. For example the energy is there affecting people whether they know it or not, but if you can FEEL it or sense it, imagine how much quicker you can clear it or heighten it?

Using candles, bells, sage or even high vibrating music (rock music by the way works well) will shift and heighten energy blocks and vortex's. If there is anything else there simply use the following tool.

<u>To shift stagnant or non physical energy from your home or workplace:</u>

1) Ensure you are grounded, protected and calm.

2) 'See' a white shaft of light come down into the centre of ALL the areas or rooms you want to clear.

3) Ask Archangel Michael & Archangel Gabriel to 'heighten and protect and clear the energy in every room and every energetic realm within the rooms '.

4) Now, see the roof 'lifting off' and ask God herself (or himself) or creator to 'please come in bless, protect, remove and deflect anything that is not of your highest and purest nature thank you and amen'.

5) See beautiful gold sparkly energy coming down and bathing each room in golden light.

6) For anything 'else' see a stairway of gold forming in each m and now ask 'dearest archangel Michael to escort all and any grounded spirits and entities over to the realms of light never to return again'.

7) Now this is the fun part 'see' a great big golden vacuum, a heavenly Henry Dyson if you will, and ask Michael to clear 'all vortex's all portals and clusters and imprints leaving only light and please leave a shield of protection around and through everything through which only love can penetrate'.

8) Light a candle if you can for a few moments, it helps the old stuff be vaporised, or leave a stone or rock near the door. The earth will absorb anything unwanted or not of the light into herself, leaving your workspace or home space clear and beautiful to be in.

Remember, being an empath is part of being human. Understanding when it's affecting you doesn't mean anything's wrong or that you have to stop. If you want to develop your gifts and understand your life purpose and hear higher guidance it's important to be able to sense what energy is a match and what energy isn't, it's also important to love yourself for the sensitive empathic being you are, and knowing that ultimately you are always safe and you can call on your angels at any time for quick protection and assistance.

The Angels Say; 'An easy way of understanding if you are affected by cords is to spend a few moments taking a few deep breaths, and now ask the question 'am I corded and to whom' see where your mind naturally goes too. The shoulders and neck are common as is the stomach and heart. Simply ask us or Michael to remove what no longer serves and enjoy your day.

Chapter 11

WHAT TO DO WHEN IT'S ALL GOING WRONG

The one thing the angels wanted me to convey, is the difference between our understanding of what's going on now and soul level understanding. They also want me to provide some troubleshooting tips that you can use to get back onto your path quickly and be the amazing soul you are.

Because you are part of a soul group, and have soul contracts with family members and friends. It is inevitable that their growth and their circumstances can also affect yours. This doesn't always make expanding and making progress fast. It does certainly provide us with opportunities to deepen our connection with 'all that is' and ultimately be the light beings we truly are.

When things' go wrong' from a human perspective or 'stop working' from a soul perspective you are just where you were designed to be.

The angels perspectives on lack and abundance

'There is no lack', is what the angels tell me. There is only a perception of it. We were designed to always expand. This means we always need more 'reasons' to grow. Sometimes the very 'lack' that we are perceiving is the very subject that will mean that we learn something new, seek a new direction or ask for assistance.

As humans, we knew that 'more' was going to be a series of desires that could never be fulfilled. The point of the journey is the journey not the destination. We also have the ability to manifest what we require.

Now, the angels asked me to put that word 'require' instead of 'need'. Some of us think we NEED more money, more love, more freedom, yet our soul who has our blueprint for this life knows what we require to fulfil our lessons. Now, that may not seem 'fair' when you see 'not such good people' attracting money easily, winning the lottery or just falling on their feet. But here's the thing, when you understand that the soul wants to be paid In growth and knowledge, then you, or this aspect of you, can also have all the abundance, money, happiness, love, and fun that you think your being is denied.

Your soul knows that 'whilst you here' you have certain contracts and lessons to learn and a certain amount of knowledge to absorb. Your soul also knows that there will be distractions, tests, new desires borne, and new themes started or to be continued at another time. Put simply your soul knows you will be like a kid in a sweetshop, spoilt for choice.

Not only is the world abundant, the universe is abundant! Now I'm not a prosperity coach and I won't tell you that your patterns are the 'only reason you don't have X amount of money or success' because I don't think that's actually accurate. What I am told is that when you were living in pure euphoria (ie you were DEAD) you didn't consider earthly and material circumstances as being your priority. Believe it or not the lessons you are finding so troublesome now, (which are also the very opportunities that will bring you the particular brand of 'more' that you want) are the doorways to attracting what your personality thinks it needs.

The angels suggest you spend some time connecting with your eternal and higher self, who in it's wisdom, along with your team of guides and your soul council, decreed what level of challenges your should experience.

When you connect with your soul, either in meditation or through contemplation, you will connect to true abundance. Do this often enough and 'earthly abundance' will start to find you.

All of the clearings, all of the 'pattern ridding' products and readings I have seen and yes performed, do not 'clear' what is needed to help you expand, yet, by connecting to your eternal and wiser self, you will not identify so much with the earthly limits you are facing now.

Now I LOVE the law of attraction, I adore Abraham Hicks, however I also see people that are trying to 'be happy all the time' tying themselves up in knots when nothing changes. The angels are sharing with me as I write that truly you can't kick what you set In motion, whether you did it by accident (your point of attraction and taking on the beliefs of others) or whether you did it by design (you wrote it in your blue print). You have to 'get on board' fully and wholeheartedly with what 'is' even if every part of your body and mind kicks against it.

The ONLY way of attracting your specific version of 'more', is not to feel that you need it. In other words to 'already have it' so 'more' comes in. The other part of this is to give your attention to the lessons and the growth that your soul decreed you should learn. Rather than beating up on yourself, or anyone else for 'what is', accept it. Become at one 'with what you are and where you are' and slowly, and yes it is slowly, you will realise that these very 'lacking' circumstances are going to be the reason you expand. It may mean that:

1) You retrain and learn some new skills, which will lead you into a new realm of work.

2) You take responsibility for the money you have and use it more wisely.

3) You get advice/assistance on practical matters and feel good really proud of yourself for doing so.

4) You accept your physical or emotional situation to the point where you are slowly ready to expand in other ways; this may mean using your mind more than your body, or using your physical relationships as tools to grow.

The one message here is that abundance surrounds you. But the only way it can come to you is if your consciousness grows. If your physical personality itself grows, (perhaps through challenge and perhaps through experimentation) and then the higher part of you grows. When the higher part of you grows and you regularly tap into this part of you, then your life grows. Abundance grows and so does every other good thing.

One final message is this, what you need and what you require are different. When you require something you can have many other things that you would love and will enjoy, and they will come because you are doing what you are contracted to do.

When you need something, it's because something inside isn't healing isn't expanding and you are mistaking the external (even in relationships) from being able to keep you happy. When you take back all of your power, and understand that even if you do not know the end result the fastest way to manifest abundance is to be totally and entirely connected to the non physical eternally abundant part of you. Then, everything you ever wanted but do not need and also what you require can begin to show up.

The angels have also asked me to mention that the universe knows and feels everything. So it will be aware that you are 'trying to be happy until … … ' and the 'until' is what it thinks you want, and so with baited breath you wait … and wait …

Stop waiting, start living and focus on your abundance of ALL good things. Look at everything you have learnt so far, look at everything you have expanded through so far. And now just for a moment FEEL how amazing it is to know that you are strong, and capable and able to create a much higher version. You're amazingly abundant because you are also a creator, and You created you.

Sheelagh Maria says: 'Of course you want to know why certain things happened. You want to know why you were born? But the thing is nobody is keeping it from you. The whole purpose truly for every one of us is to discover why we are here through our relationships and our growth. Rest assured not one person, the angels tell me, have gone home without fulfilling their purpose. Some people have very different ideas of what a purpose is. For example when mass tragedy happens it's often to raise awareness of a certain issue or those souls volunteered to leave so the earth could purge through them and ascend and so help the whole of humanity. No life is ever wasted and no person is ever fully bad or good. We are all a part of a whole and every one of us bad good and ugly pure sinner and saint is all connected to the innate goodness of the universe.

Chapter 12

LIFE PURPOSE LONG TERM

T he angels want you to think about where you are now and where you would love to be. They say if you have a 'dream' or a 'target' but you feel it's a million light years away, it's likely that you have become 'infected' by 'world energy'. World or mass consciousness energy basically makes it difficult to believe or see 'how' you are able to move through blocks and become happy, successful and abundant.

Your life purpose is always meant to make you feel good. It's meant to be a variety of what you are learning, where you are, sharing what you are teaching, and what you are 'living' right now. It's not a job title, or in particular your spiritual ability, but your job and your spiritual ability can be a big part of your life purpose.

Your life purpose is also at play at every moment. There is no moment 'ever' whether you are in a body or not. That you are not living or moving along your souls path. That's because you are a soul and its impossible not to grow it's in the very nature of the 'material' you are made up of.

If you perceive that your life purpose will start 'when' something occurs, you can actively block it from coming in, so the angels are asking you to understand that those 'dreams' and 'targets' need to be part of but not all that you consider to make up your overall life purpose.

Where you are now is part of where you are going

Do you have a target or a goal that you seem to be thwarted when it comes to moving towards? Is this goal or target connected to money? Or relationships? The angels are saying when you are not moving forwards towards a goal and it feels as though you are stuck in quick sand, it is likely that 'world energy', 'community energy' or 'family energy' is blocking you. It can feel as though wherever you advertise your services, wherever you go to find a new soul mate, wherever you apply for a job, you are getting bounced back – but here's the thing, it's PART of your life purpose to go through this.

The angels say it "can mean you are not supposed to have something if it becomes a huge struggle" but in the end you are being guided to 'check' your vibration, and what's 'gotten stuck' in order for you to clear it. Then things will start flowing again. It's part of your life purpose even to be reading this book and to understand 'when' you are 'blocked' and 'how' to get clear.

Where you are now is the doorway to where you want to go, and when it seems as though things keep going wrong your angels are saying you've skipped a step. It may be that you have all the 'real world' qualifications for the job or the relationship, but it is likely that you have some patterns or beliefs that are strongly affecting your true alignment to that experience. They are advising you to learn how to clear your energy from all those different areas and then, after nurturing yourself, move forward once more.

Your life purpose will affect other people's paths

You know you are on your life path when your choices are affecting others around you. Sometimes it may be in a challenging way, ie. They don't want to grow and don't see why you should 'make them'. (Of course their higher self and yours designed it that way) Or you may find that they start learning new things, attracting new experiences and you may even find the 'level of' the people around you goes up as well.

It is also completely normal for friends' even relatives to drop away for a time, or for good. As you step onto your true life path your vibration goes UP. As a result of this some relationships and some interactions will change, and at some point they are no longer needed. This doesn't mean you are doing anything 'wrong' quite the opposite, it's just the 'speed of the soul' is too different between you to continue.

Your life purpose will also highlight to others how they can also expand and grow. So don't be surprised if what looks like a mid life crisis or a breakdown is actually a breakthrough for some people. Your angels want you to know that 'being selfish' is just a perception we are all here to really expand and that means even those of you that feel more comfortable with 'staying the same..

Your life theme affects what you can manifest

Your life theme and your life lessons will affect what you are able to manifest with your happy thoughts. If you are barking up the wrong tree you can bark till the full moon comes out, it won't make a difference.

Your life theme for example, if it was 'harmony' would probably not catapult you to a muti-millionaire status. Because you are here to balance the books with everyone around you. Someone with a life theme of 'adventure' may struggle to manifest a long term family and home life because they are meant at soul level to be out there going for it. A life theme for example of perseverance can make building a business quickly (even if you follow all the marketing plans and all the get rich quick schemes) a challenge. It's important once you understand what your life theme is to clear your vibration up enough so that you can do what you agreed to do and then 'you can manifest and do other stuff too'.

Chapter 13

WHAT IS MY LIFE THEME

The angels tell me this is very simple, it's basically speaking the 'subject matter' and the 'stance' you are taking through out your lives. The subject matter is going to be something that has always 'been around you'. I have listed a few but there are numerous variations.

If you are clairsentient you can tune into your heart and ask your team (we suggest either your Guardian angel or Archangel Michael as you will feel their guidance easily) if you are highly empathic or clairvoyant we would suggest using a pendulum and if you are clair audient then ask and see what you are told.

Life Themes Section 1 – Service this is your 'why', this is why you have the lessons you have and how you personally benefit from them. When you identify this you understand more of where you are in your over all souls evolution.

Healer: You are here to heal yourself through this theme and then others.

Martyr: You are here to experience giving at a high level and then valuing self.

Teacher: You have achieved a higher status in other lifetimes and now through your example you teach.

Pupil: You are learning wonderful new ways of growing.

Ambassador: You have already 'got this down' and now you act as a way shower to others.

Catalyst: You are experiencing changes and are the causes of change for yourself and others.

Observer: You are here to take notes energetically and feed this information back to your soul group.

Experimenter: You are trying different stances for size and finding what works.

Master: You are completed in this lesson and now are ready to act as an advocate a teacher and mentor for others your experiences may be harsher or more protracted as you enter Master Soul status.

Life Themes Section 2: This is what you are being encouraged to learn and understand through the life you have.

Trust: You are learning all facets of trusting others, when to trust, when to step back and when to trust your self.

Self Love: You are learning to step away from the opinions of others and understand the amount of love you feel for, is what will be reflected back this can take some time.

Perseverance: Just because things haven't worked out doesn't mean they won't, you are asked to keep going and keep being aware of how far you have come.

Detachment: This is important if you have in previous lives or in this one gotten hung up on where or what others are deciding or feeling, it is also important to understand the universe will take your feelings about others as being yours. Detachment allows you to receive more and struggle less.

Patience: You may feel as though things are never going to change, but thine timing and divine timing are different things, you're being asked here to please see the benefits of going with the flow.

Fun and laughter: You may have many reasons not to celebrate and it may seem selfish or not 'the right thing to do' to some but you have so much to celebrate. Heaven itself is light and loving and you cannot manifest anything worthwhile through heaviness and lower energy this is your invitation to let more light into your world and see how quickly everything changes.

Inner connection/self belief: This is about identifying with the internal rather than the external. The external only changes when our knowledge of the internal is strong. You are being asked to discard anything which is outside of you and appreciate how perfect and unique you and your circumstances are for growth.

Wisdom: You are being asked to 'see and feel' beyond the issues around you. See what others are mirroring for you to learn and grow through, see where others are frightened to grow. Your role in this is to simply be aware of your higher guidance and where invited allow others to grasp the same truth.

Compassion: This means you are being asked to see beyond what yanks at your mind and heart and have compassion for where others are on their journey. It doesn't mean capitulation or sacrifice. It does mean being in allowance of yourself and your own feelings too. We are not responsible for others but we are responsible for how to interact with others and having compassion for yourself is above all the biggest component of your growth.

Life Theme Section 3 : This is where you are living a theme from multiple lives. When we have a lesson, we are expected to experience it from all standpoints. Victim, observer, master, healer, aggressor etc. It is not that you are considered 'bad' if you are at a point where you are living a lesson from a different standpoint to 'light' it is part of our growth and we have all been all things.

There is a famous song it goes like this 'I'm a bitch, I'm a lover, I'm a child, I'm a mother, I'm a sinner I'm a saint – I do not need to change ... ' This is the angels sharing that nobody is any 'better' than anyone else. Even if from your own personal standpoint you think 'that person' is 'bad' because they have done or responded to something in a different or 'lower' way, they may actually experience great growth and be filled with remorse or a desire to give back further down the line. So 'do not judge another's path' for you have been there too.

We all have 'dark lifetimes' and we all have 'black and white lifetimes'. We also have lifetimes where we have 'turned from the light' and are 'turning to the light. God and creator is 'evil' as well as 'good'. There are dark archangels without whom the world could not provide us polarity and of course 'light archangels', they all have their place in creation. We can even have 'dark guides' who guide us through a part of our growth that is needed for us to turn to the light. So wife beaters, criminals, people that manipulate and cause havoc are also teaching lessons at soul level. It is all part of the whole picture.

In this section please use your discretion it is in response to the current lesson you are living through rather than being a description of your whole journey. Although remember some do carry their 'labels' for the whole journey. For example once upon a time (as you will see in my bio) I considered myself to be a victim and then a pupil and now a teacher. In another lesson I will be all three again.

At This Stage In Your Current Life Lesson Are You?

A victim: This is necessary to get to a point where you will acknowledge your desire to live in a different way. It's a powerful stage because it takes a lot of courage not to blame outside circumstances that can be heartbreaking to the naked eye, and to take responsibility for your point of attraction.

An aggressor: This doesn't make you a bad person, it simply means you are feeling scared or extremely frustrated and are sending your anger 'out' instead of releasing it and accepting responsibility. You can be an aggressor in a 'texting war' or even in judging a single mum. It's all relative. The reason the angels want you to know this is so you can release your lower feelings and transform into the loving being you truly are.

An accessory: This is when you are either helping someone 'stay with their status' for your benefit or through your eyes, there's. You may have a friend who's been in a domestic violent situation and you really 'uphold' her status as victim. Of course this doesn't help her and it also means you are using your status as a 'helper' to prevent stepping into your power. It's also the case where we are scared to tackle the aggressor for fear of the attention coming our way.

An observer: This is where you are seeing what is going on and staying firmly out of it. Yet part of your growth is to step in and protect the victim, but not take sides against the aggressor. It's a profound role if used properly as it is one many masters have. Which is ensuring all parties accept their growth as needed for the expansion of the whole.

A 'stool pigeon': Okay this is the angels language for a fall guy. This is where you are at the centre of a dispute or disagreement or are the subject of everyone's attention. You are being 'used as fodder' and as a target for peoples anger/concern/ pity. Now the thing is, with this it can feel really good or really not good because it doesn't help you or them.

Your role in this is to extract yourself and to understand you don't need to be the centre of lower energy or people misusing their focus for you to be unique and important in your own right. It's time to find your voice and state clearly that you are the creator of your experience and give them their power back as well.

The coddler: Okay so this is the angels way of saying you are taking on the responsibility for someone else, and you are doing it with misguided good intentions. You may be feeding the other person 'reasons' why they should play it safe, shouldn't take a risk or should stay where they are. But ultimately it's because if they grow or change your security feels at risk. This is a role often played by mothers and fathers but spouses can also do this, and it doesn't accelerate anyone's path.

The runaway: This is you if you are burying your head in the sand or diverting your attention from what the real issue is. An example would be someone who does not want to admit that they are scared or who does not want to admit that there is an issue within a relationship. Yet when you do, it can be sorted and resolved and true peace and contentment can come in again.

The Protagonist: This is you if you feel very strongly about someone else's story. You may take their vantage point for them and feel overly wronged or overly empathic for them. You may seek to balance the scales of justice or worse send judgement towards another like the runaway. What you are doing is looking to curry favour by upholding one perspective that is not yours and does not empower the other person to step into their truth, it's also an avoidance tactic for you.

And is different things to different people and in the end wastes a lot of energy and a lot of focus on things that would have resolved on their own. Funnily enough someone who fears being 'the black sheep' often takes this stance. They get their identity by keeping everyone else happy. The angels are asking you now to remember that your purpose is not to fulfil everyone else's growth. Your purpose is to fulfil your growth, let your light shine and let your true path be revealed.

Life Themes Section 4: This is the most basic life themes section. It tells you the SUBJECT you came here to share and evolve through. It is put simply the ENERGY rather than the 'title' of what you should be doing. When you look at this simply close your eyes and ask your guides to help you to see the main energy through which your life should be lived. It is a movement towards inner happiness and connection. It doesn't matter whether your are great grandmother or the CEO of a huge firm. The energy that you are here to bring through is going to come through whatever you 'do with your day.

Joy
Peace
Motivation
Honesty
Trust
Truth
Wisdom
Challenge
Change
Awareness
Enlightenment
Acceptance
Faith
Hope
Appreciation

Life Theme Section 5 Who Am I Meant To Work With?

This is the energy level you are best suited too. If you are not meant to be working with human souls it doesn't matter how long you sit in a circle for, your messages will not be as deep and meaningful. You are a vessel for your spirit, whatever job you do, but working with the correct 'grade' of energy will open your life path and your life gifts in a much faster way.

Am I meant to work with and receive guidance from?

Devic kingdom: Fairies, woodland and flower spirits, nature and elementals.

Animal kingdom: Including deceased animals power animals and totem animals.

Magical realms: – Mermaids, dolphins, unicorns' dragons. (Not just with oracle cards but channelling or healing)

Spirit guides

Ascended spirit guides: These bring through specialist subject matter such as healing psychic surgery philosophy

Ascended masters

Angels & archangels

Star beings : Often don't have names.

Group beings: Again don't have names.

Goddess or deity energy: Such as the Egyptian energies and the energies of Bridget Fiona etc

Shamanic energy

Celtic Druidic /Wiccan energy

House consciousness

Business consciousness

Prosperity consciousness

Loved ones in spirit

Human souls

Children in spirit

Wise one energy

So you see there are a huge variety of beings you can work with. It's time for you to open your intuition so that you can receive guidance and love from your team in wonderful ways, ways that will really speed up lighten and expand your path.

Chapter 14

YOUR MISSION NOW, SHOULD YOU CHOOSE TO ACCEPT IT?

So you have got a fair bit of information regarding living your life purpose. The angels would love you to know that they are practical not fluffy and willing to assist you in every way. Very often I am told that people are blocked, or not getting answers. The angels say that the original blueprint for you, set by your soul is the reason it can feel this way. Remember you came here to experience the spectrum of emotions and experiences. The soul does not judge any growth as wasted as it all helps and therefore the source for the universe to expand.

It can be hard to understand why good things happen to bad people. Why bad things happen to the very best of people, but remember this we have all been all things in other times.

When you are not experiencing what you feel you should, it's because you're not a match for it yet. Perhaps it's not listed on your manifesto as being part of your path.

The angels would like you to remember:

1) Your souls purpose includes your natural gifts, tendencies, quirks and responses, the good, bad and ugly.

2) Your souls purpose should 'flow,' it shouldn't be stop and start, stuck, or blocked. If this is occurring you are likely convinced that something is meant for you that simply is not. The soul does not judge your human yearnings, yet it is not pulsed when you place focus on something that isn't part of your path.

3) Listen to what your intuition rather than your emotions tell you. Put simply, we usually know what direction we should be heading in even if we don't have an action, or an outcome to name at this time.

4) Your next step is often smaller and yet more significant than you think. Something as simple as admitting you were wrong, or loving yourself more, being compassionate with someone for where they are, or stepping back and getting another perspective can be what's needed to get things flowing again. Flow don't force is the golden rule!

5) When you are focused on a big outcome or a big event it's hard to see it ever transpiring with the set of circumstances we have now. Often investing in ourselves, gaining advice, getting some healing, or taking some time 'out' and connecting with our inner wisdom or playing, will allow the energy to settle, clear and strengthen so it becomes obvious to you what your next priority should be.

6) The angels really can help you and I want to take a moment to recap on 'how'.

The angels can help you by:

1) Bringing your energy into alignment with the outcome that is right for you, now. If you are genuinely blocked because of other peoples energy, and you do not have the time or money to get professional help healing or clearing, asking the angels for a

clearing on abundance, a clearing on health or a clearing around relationships will always work. Simply ask! Don't worry about how. Spending some time quietly focusing on the breath allows the healing to be done and also for the energies to settle so that the new energy can flow in. This usually takes around 2 weeks.

2) Helping you to be aware of the thought patterns that are keeping you where you are. They can't heal you without your express permission, and even if they do the way you are thinking about things is what's bringing the evidence in. Asking the angels to highlight to you a perspective that allows healing is brilliant because if you have a viewpoint that allows fear to settle and then be released then new energy and resources will follow.

3) Bringing your time line into its highest vibration. So often we fall into old patterns, when something happens that hits a sore spot from the past (or even a past life) we can slip backwards down to another time and place where we were not so aware.

Asking the angels to bring for example your financial energy into it's highest vibration, means that if you are going to be very well off in say ten years, that energy level can be accessed now. Or if you were emotionally very happy and settled in your thirties, you can replicate that energy now so that the circumstances over time flow in.

4) Ensuring you are in the right place at the right time. Often it is a chance meeting, an epiphany in the company of someone else or an article that you read is that informs you of what is your next step or right move. Asking the angels to help you be where you need to be and do what you are supposed to do but then relaxing, means you don't have to be on 'high alert' for signs. Just follow your nose and affirm 'everything is working out for me every day' and believe it when you say it.

5) Writing down an affirmation and putting it on your wall and saying it every time you enter the room will not only change the energy in the room but brings the energy into you aura. So for example if on your bathroom wall you have some paper that says 'I lovingly attract abundance in unlimited ways; every time you say this you sow a seed that has to flower. As long as you smile and mean it at that moment. Chanting it verbatim when you clearly feel something else won't help, or a hot bath, cup of tea or chat with your best friend will work better for you.

Your Angels Say

That your mission, should you choose to accept it, is to expand one day, one hour, one moment at a time. It's to do your best to understand when you are playing smaller than you meant to. To take those 'risks' that can and will lead to a broader experience for you. To give thanks for all your relationships and to remain grateful for the contribution every one in your life has made no matter how things stand between you now.

Put simply, your life purpose is to show love towards others but honour yourself and put those boundaries down when you need too. Coming from the heart does not mean capitulation or sacrifice. It means knowing that deep down although people project, they are challenging you to be more, feel more and know more what is right for you.

Your mission, should you choose to accept it, is not impossible. Highly probable and absolutely inevitable. Your angels, your higher self and your soul mates are all part of the wonderful tapestry, that you, a piece of god, a treasured light worker, a beautiful spark of light, made in the likeness of the creator, will fulfil perfectly along with your angels at every turn.

With love magic and infinite blessings

Sheelagh and your angels

Printed in the United States
By Bookmasters